AFFORDABLE WONDERS

BY

IAN SOWTON

Order this book online at www.trafford.com
or email orders@trafford.com

Most Trafford titles are also available at major online book retailers.

Permissions: The line from "Ends of the Earth", from *FOX: POEMS 1998-2000*
By Adrienne Rich. Copyright © 2001 by Adrienne Rich. Used by
permission of the author and W.W. Norton & Company Inc..

"Bruckner", by Denise Levertov, from *SANDS OF THE WELL*.
Copyright © 1994, 1995, 1996 by Denise Levertov. Reprinted by
permission of New Directions Publishing Corporation.

Printed in the United States of America.

ISBN: 978-1-4269-3139-0 (sc)

Trafford rev. 02/10/2011

www.trafford.com

North America & international
toll-free: 1 888 232 4444 (USA & Canada)
phone: 250 383 6864 ♦ fax: 812 355 4082

for Fran, as always

and

Merle Sowton, in memoriam

TABLE OF CONTENTS
[* Notes pp. 196-199]

v

OBSEQUIES

PSALMS

AUTHOR'S NOTE: This volume comprises a number of recent poems together with selections from the author's previous collections of poems, ***Intricate Armada*** (2005) and ***Imagining Sisyphus Happy*** (2006). A number of poems included from those two earlier books have been revised—some slightly, others considerably, and a few radically. *I.S.*

ADDENDUM TO *A PRIMER OF*
MARINE DIALECTS

Among other things Shakespeare was
phonologically apt in oceanic dialects.
Thus Timon, a liminal shoreline chap:
                    ...say to Athens,
Timon hath made his everlasting mansion
Upon the beached verge of the salt flood,
Who once a day with his embossed froth
The turbulent surge shall cover.
catches an anapestic swirl, accent of sea
as restless elegist. But then Alcibiades
re-hears that tone of turbulence—
                    ...yet rich conceit
Taught thee to make vast Neptune weep for ay
On thy low grave, on faults forgiven
as an assuaging dialect of calm iambics.
Or there's Dickens and, say, his Dombeys
with the river rolling through the city of their lives
 towards the sea. Sea with its "waves
that are hoarse with repetition of their mystery."
'*The sea, Floy, what is it that it keeps on saying?*''
She told him that it was only the noise of the
rolling waves. 'Yes, yes,' he said, 'But I know that
they are always saying something. Always the same thing.'
In Dickens' colossal phrase book of the human spirit,
where the ocean always puts the accent—
what it's hoarse with insisting on, often
to deaf ears—is human loving-kindness.

Or listen to Yeats listening:
how marvellously sharp of ear to catch
That dolphin-torn, that gong-tormented sea...,
that accent of the sea's amazement

1

at the depth, fraughtness and, yes,
high perils of its furies and complexities.

To descend from such sublimities:
By grace of echo-sounding wizardry
I too, propped up in Intensive Care,
have listened (in my shoreline way
of wet inside and dry outside)
to my tiny tides ebb and flow.
In their chuckling whorls and gurgles
up and down the grottos of my heart,
I think now that perhaps I overheard
in the salt dialect of some distant surf—
accents, amazement-hushed, ushering
a primal lurch into parlous amphibious life.

ASCENSIONTIDE

A pair of fashionably too-large sneakers
sits empty in the lamplight on our lawn.
Practising round-the-compass jumps
from standing start, Orlando
has just twirled himself right out
of his shoes
   He's reeling off into the shadows
and there they sit, empty
in the evening lamplight, managing to look
both bereft and poised

For the split of a second as laughter
ambushes me, I intuit ascension: divinity
(God must be twelve if she's a day)
leaping—an ecstasy of energy—
right out of its incarnate sneakers

And coming back down, of course,
there being the matter of gravity's tax
on all ascents
   But do not, Goddess,
assess his, or any child's, jumps
at too steep a rate
   Let them descend
the stairs of their young mornings
with no black hole of hunger sucking
that divinity, that rapturous twirl of energy
   Let them fall back in their shoes of body
with no landmines chewing on their tibias
   Let them breathe inalienable welcome
as in and out as ordinary air

RESOLUTION

New Year 2008.
     Whereas: like happiness
miracles have this trick of revealing them-
selves after the event
     Resolved: this Lent
I will abstain from disenchantment,
   world weariness, all customary
   cynicisms
      and remembering
   that garden confluence
   of miracle—quizzical grackle
      white peonies
      Imogen running
I will assemble an enchantment-
prone brownbag lunch, lay
a spell of grace on it and climb
into this shiny loan of hours
hoping, no, expecting to glimpse
a miracle, maybe even two
in the rear view mirror of my day

MIDWIFE'S CAROL

The birth itself was not too hard
good presentation, fine strong mum
but my dear it was a circus
I thought that half the town had come
  wash him clean, wipe him dry
  hush you, shush you, rock-a-bye

There were these shepherds who burst in
my dear they said a talking light
told them to come and pay respects—
kneeling they were to that wee mite
  wash him clean, wipe him dry
  hush you, shush you, rock-a-bye

He's breathing well, the cord's tied off
her afterbirth's come free my dear
when three fine scholar blokes squeeze in
saying a star has brought them here
  wash him clean, wipe him dry
  hush you, shush you, rock-a-bye

You selling tickets then? I said,
buzz off you lot and let her rest
and they did, too, leaving presents—
rich stuff my dear, the very best
  wash him clean, wipe him dry
  hush you, shush you, rock-a-bye

All that public to and fro-ing
she watches as it comes and goes
with him tucked, dear, in a manger
pulled from under the donkey's nose
  wash him clean, wipe him dry
  hush you, shush you, rock-a-bye

Winter solstice it was my dear
shivery cold and animal stink
worship, palaver, gifts and all—
what was going on do you think?
wash him clean, wipe him dry
hush you, shush you, rock-a-bye

CHRISTMAS EVE IN ST. LUCIA

Holiday as holy-day:
strange as two magi without a third
we search for the Nativity until
an auspicious streetlamp playing star
lights us to this moment numinous
with best of vocations, host and guest:

dusk and a woman chatting by her car,
we ask the way and she accepts
the offer from this holy night to be a host,
drives us, angel in a British Ford,
three blocks to St Andrews door,
leaves us with strict directions to return
not by the way we came
but that way, do you see? that other way

We go in bearing our gift of guesthood

As liturgies of carol unfold familiar
suburbs of childhood Bethlehems
we suddenly are a kind of host
to these new neighbours, giving
in our half-thawed winter voices
substance to that mythic cold which
we dispel with them in ceremonious songs
of warm Word rising, shining now
on every shore of a december world

Caribbean lilts of greeting chime
gentle in our ears as we set out in holy night
hotelward by, do you see? that other way.

CHRISTMAS TIDINGS

Going flow-wise down Jasper Avenue
(I have measured out my life in traffic lights)
scratching myself and bleeding oil,
I saw John the Baptiser's head stream
in boreal light, heard it cry Sin! Repentance!
(there being only one more shopping day etc)
to Canada while his lost Salome shivered
through the terror of her dance in dreams

On guard O Canada for you, I caper
        frozen while you lie pacific
to your newfound toes, digesting
        news to pulp and burping NAFTAs.
Why me? yourself so guarded that no one
        can peep up your Sunday shore line
unless they're OK with the CIA
        and white as chastity. Bashfully reserving
everything from judgement to First Nations,
        you're so on guard you need Liquor Boards
to tell you that you're wicked

When I or any of your lovers
        come calling on you religiously
or stiff with learning, you serve up
        separate schools and bankrupt universities;
when we push in, reeking with justice,
        you shut those glaciers that were your eyes
and think of flags or royal commissions;
        when we tickle you, you giggle liberally
but if we really sport and squeeze
        you progressively conserve the game
to simulated thrills fake as any spin
        doctored in our PMO's winter wonderland

Won't anything but profits turn you on
              and thaw you out? Where are the fires
that forged those passionate Cascades
              for your collarbone? Look at you:
so numb you can't feel your common-
              wealth leaking through your tax cuts;
blowing your nose on *Le Devoir* and stomping
              the Québec flag to warm your anglo chilblains;
guts rumbling with E-colied drinking water,
              mangy clear cuts tufting out your hair
and half the buying power of us sewn up
              in that golden girdle round your sweet Toronto

Listen, you frosting on the Great American Cake,
              you Auditor General's worst nightmare come
                                          true,
I prophesy you cities dying of development,
              layoffs, convenient bankruptcies, neocon men,
governments as business agencies,
              idiot slogans on parade with conflicts
of interest scurrying and squeaking underfoot.
              What if you forgot to blush at a real idea
and edited yourself out of your delusional
              reality shows? Or hoisted your skirt of prairie
above its bottom line to let an actual feeling,
              a frisson of justice, tap dance on your haunch?

I tell you there'd be a happening:
              you'd become a thing to thank God on—
Innu surf riding in Hudson's Bay,
              Alliance-Tory MPs reciting Schüssler Fiorenza,
massed beavers whistling tourists in and out
              to Handel's *Water Music*. We'd bounce
your huge laurentian mattress like puck,
              melt your knees to milk and maple syrup.

9

Warm as Cuba your whooping cranes, turned gold,
would sing to lords and ladies of Tamiscaming
of what is passed, or passing, or to come

All this I saw and heard: the Baptist's head
(there being only one more shopping day etc)
howling after the lost body of his love
but lights changed, his mouth went yellow
and started calling "Cars love Shell".
No glory of the lord shone round about
so back into my goodwill trance I fell
flow-wise home across the North Saskatchewan
all unbaptised and far, oh interminably
far far beneath the stately conversation
of auroras in the holy arctic skies.

WINTER INSCAPE

In hindsight one knows
it's ill advised to go windsurfing
down the back of indian summer—
el Niño's asthma is too unpredictable:
       there I was, bouncing along
minding my own balance
when I was wheezed shank
       over chin bone
right through the front grill
of this damn white whale
          Useless
to point out (breath steaming)
that I am unmorselly from way back

They say the function of shivering
is to keep warm— if I could be heard
above the clatter of my eye-teeth
I would tell that to the Snow Fairy

Take an inside look at the ribs
of this beast: like a frost bitten grove
of anxious verbs
         bending stiffly
over dropped off nouns

Out. I want out.
         Yellow me with bile,
make me make him bilious,
make him spew me praising
on the shores of Spring

IN THIS MOST INTRICATE ARMADA
for Fran

In this most intricate armada of them all
fleeting it along, in tow, or wallowing—
a million courses for a million Indies set—
how best to find the right flotilla, the safety
of dry decks from that last aloneness of a raft?
how best to tune in on some length of wave
that brings me speech against this hurricane of voice?
how best to know which Neptune plots my straits and
$\qquad\qquad\qquad\qquad\qquad\qquad$ narrows?
Captain captain what of all these waves?
Sailor, to ride or to drown in the take of a breath

The time and times this body's creaky ship
meets others infinitely sovereign and unknown—
keeled in strange yards—passing, crossing wakes
with mere red of nod or green of wave until
they're lost in lazy hazes of acquaintance;
or leaves the lanes well shipped for meeting,
avoids the current of a likely rendezvous
and lays that smokescreen of approaching unaware
Captain captain what of nameless bows?
Sailor, to fool them in case they're the raider you fear

Here some cruise ship, ensigns all come-hithering
yet numinous with mystery, parts the horizon
like Venus rising from the foam—all chaste allure—
but any spyglass eye can see the bloody scuppers,
seagulls scrapping in the seethy wake for hearts;
there, beaten by some unimaginable storm,
its lifeboat of a laugh stove in,
a tramp goes staggered by my hasty wash
Captain captain what of all these skeletons?
Sailor, to weave nightmares on when you're snug in
$\qquad\qquad\qquad\qquad\qquad\qquad$ *berth*

What, brave boys, to do when well-found craft are
                              battered
into foolery? for in this dream of fleets
soundlessly lips move, the friendly hail whipped off
in a gale of platitudes. Heavy the heart's anchor
sinks in unfathomable groping for a hold,
while rockets of a desperate glance burst once
to hiss out in the brine of elseward looking eyes
and, in the very take of bearing, we're apart and lost
Captain captain what of all this fog?
Sailor, to keep star-maps bright in the eye of your mind

Every saint of sailors bless me! what to do
with drifting hulks doldrumed in a mortal calm
when there's not a puff, not a pint of fuel to spare?
if, though we pass close as touching, hawsers snap
and to the spinning wish of helm there comes no turn?
if *Reverse* clangs on the bridge but never down
where ego's great one-willpowered engines run?
if O Christ for your own self I could not put about?
Captain captain what of all this speed?
Sailor, to try one more time to catch nightfall napping

In this crazed network of static garble code
suddenly a signal, on my wavelength, in the clear.
And after so much meeting to then tacking fro
here is the seven oceans' prize fabulously
holding the same course as I. She, yes, heaves to
and welcomes boarders, party to sweet piracy.
Bodies for chart, looks open as north for compass
we steer in close formation for love's squadron
Captain captain what of that far coast?
Sailor, the prospect of waking in harbour one day

ENGAGEMENT

no phrase-book loquacities:
      desire unfolds silent
in each other's awestruck presence

no bridal catalogues:
      one another's body
is what shyly we begin to wear

no wedding special:
      two bowls of soup, a pot
of sacramental Chinese tea

no vows yet:
      for now
hands infant-new to touch
      pledge under naked eyes

EROS DISCLOSED

My dear, we owe it to all poor students
to tell them where else to find true love
in Metropolitan Toronto besides tourist
brochures and the bushes of High Park

They should think Royal Ontario Museum:
display case of ancient roman coins where,
though you look to my surreptitious eyes
more unattainable than Caesar's ward,
Farraday himself could not be managing
the charge between us better
                                              for me
no matching of imperial Trajan's beak,
no wreath of laurel on my ill groomed pate
but I looked, so you say later, seriously honest

Or take the lecture rooms of said ROM:
art and archaeology of ancient Egypt,
all those serene profiles, yours most elegant—
beautiful as fifty pharaohs' wives—being
discreetly studied by leftover light from slides
but you knew, so you say later, where I was looking

SOUNDS AND WEIGHTS

Sick at the sound of Abel's bursting skull
weeping angels turned our hearing almost off
but at some last intersection of time and space,
some inmost utmost out-of place
numinous with naggingly familiar otherness—
every shriek of agony, every whimper of distress
every forced confession's mumble
and despairing tap for help unanswered at the door,
every gasp of terror, every grumble
of every empty belly since once upon a time
sounds louder than Krakatoa's dying roar
Shocked by our weight of debt to consciousness
weeping angels tampered with the scales
but round some bend of light, some curve of space,
some utmost inmost out-of place
haunted by almost remembered dreams that died—
every breadcrumb wasted or denied
 every drop of slave blood and indentured sweat,
and pesticided egg mocking the baffled nest,
every tip-toe lie to pirouette
trippingly off any tongue since once upon a time
weighs heavier than the roots of Everest
My true love is hale and unshockable.
As injustice breeds in promiscuous quantums
I get honked off, I pray expostulatory: Look,
God, those shrieks, whimpers and confessions,
taps, gasps, each protesting belly, breadcrumbs,
 bloody drops, eggs turned to poisoned jelly,
 those lies—all must be reckoned in, accounted for!
She lets grand narratives of cosmic justice be,
 notes the world's sins and graces, knows the score,
 tends the sick, says her prayers in paintings.
 Sounds and weights of life she tunes and bears
                                        unfussily

16

IN-HOUSE GLOSA
for P.K.Page

A complete kit of muscle, vessels, bone, and skin
is packed with lore on all the best ways to proceed,
knows how to cover ground or dawdle comfortably,
can get on with repairs in peace while I'm asleep

I'm jogging through the demesne of North Toronto
a fiefdom so deep in fealty to Lord Carr that
imported nannies, a postman, are the only
other denizens afoot. There are no sidewalks.
Locomotive legs are uncool, so yesterday.
Round here each garage must have a robot live-in
for lifting, lowering, connecting vestigial shanks
to brakes and accelerators. And my dear, it's
not couth to hanker for unwithered origin—
a complete kit of muscle, vessels, bone, and skin.

During my shower (that curious noise like some
aquarium's aeration system breaking down
is me singing "*the ankle bone connected to*
th' foot bone") I wonder if developers
and town planning gurus in these parts ever heard
of feet, but then in honesty I must concede
that I, too, am among Lord Carr's old retainers,
sworn tenant faithful in my monthly tithe and rents
to Sweet Crude his steward; that my combustive steed
is packed with lore on all the best ways to proceed,

to move me around with all-in-one-piece safety
and comfort, not only from here to mundane theres
but also to Gros Morne's bare faced geologies,
or off to rough magic of Drumheller's badlands,
or Superior smacking lips of ancient rock—

all this more, or now somewhat less, affordably.
It lopes me to Prince Edward county wineries.
Carpeted Aladdin should be so mobile. Horse-
power abridges Canadian space reliably,
knows how to cover ground or dawdle comfortably.

Aeroplanes suit me alright, I save my air miles;
I like riding rails—subways, streetcars, VIA trains,
but it is between the Lord Carr's oath-binding hands
that I've contrived to place myself. Yet my arches
hanker to assert some minor independence,
nothing magna carta-ish, to serve their upkeep:
a by-law making lack of sidewalks an offence?
or an Act proclaiming Let's-Walk-a-Footpath Day?
so that my whole kit, righteous after a brisk creep,
can get on with repairs in peace while I'm asleep.

"MY DOG, BUFIK"
Glass and enamel, 1988. Jaromĭr Bychák

Bufik's back is lucent but his origin
opaque, for his pedigree is motley,
resisting all research in heraldry.
                    He is the despair
of genealogists—obviously the product
of some unsupervised orgy of imagination.

Long jaws, big pointy ears, stumpy legs,
with an expression halfway between
sublime stupidity and genius
for mischief with intent.
                    He has traversed
the whole of ugly and emerged
on other side charmingly repulsive
                    but not cuddly.

Smallish but very sturdy, he might be
a *cum laude* in martial arts dressed,
for some reason, as a slightly dangerous
clown who has marbles on toasted black
belt for breakfast;
                    for sure anyone
who grappled him would come away
with shards in tender places.

                    In his dreams
he charges up and down dunes nearly
molten hot, or along white kilometres
of perfect beach devoid of jolly people
saying "fetch!"
                    In *my* dreams
he bites everybody I don't like,

not on command—he has flunked
out of three obedience academies—
but for the heck of it because he's turned on
by my disapproving pheromones.

His grin is wonderful but in my dreams
when I say *"Survivor*!" or *"Apprentice*!"
he tries to laugh—a sound
for which the only words are
snapping crystal stemware.
                         In my dreams
when I say "Canadian identity!" he keels
over, asleep before he hits the floor. But
"National Post!" gets lots of action:
he growls, his grin takes on a cast
distinctly sinister, his paws scrabble
like hailstones rapping on a window-pane,
his mouth regrets it cannot froth.

Notwithstanding his capacity for fury
he is capable of softer feelings such as
sorrow, nostalgia tinged
                         for in my dreams
when I say "Avro Arrow!" his ceramic
tail takes on an elegiac droop and like
wet fingers rubbing fine goblet rims
he keens, mourning in a key
reminiscent of D minor.

NIGHT THOUGHTS

Counting sheep has never
done it for me—the way they shape
their noses is too fascinating

maybe I don't need as much sleep
as I used to, even the emergency
angora goats aren't working

lying here, I ponder going into
something, like, socially useful, worthy
of the Ethical Investments Registry

some enterprise for caulking
gaps in thought, for grouting
fissures in, like, social discourse

I will list my company as
Rent-A-Cliché. I will print
two-tone flyers offering discounts
for politicians, headline editors,
accredited spin-doctors
and talking heads
                      newsroom
infantry and desperate Best Men
get the introductory 2-for-1 Special

Quite frankly, it all hangs,
at the end of the day, let's face it,
on qualifying, like, for a Small Business
initiatives Loan—to be honest with you—
that is, like, the bottom line

NOW THAT I THINK OF IT

Sometimes second thoughts are like
those cancelled weekend passes
in World War 2 movies: they *might* serve
to sidestep hangovers and/or the clap,
but for sure they flatten out a Saturday.
　　　　At other times they dish out reprieves
grand as Charlemagne.
Or (not counting this as a third thought)
they can loiter fretful as debunked ghosts
in fading lavenders of regret.

❖

Every thought is always already
an afterthought, even if it's a forethought.
And remember to pronounce the right spells
over that old curse-me-down forethought—
Adam knew damn well he was in free fall
when he caught himself forethinking
the need for breeches.
　　　　　　　But thinking itself!
Oh thinking itself—when it just happens
outside the fores and afts of time—
porpoises happy through on up over
a moon-struck sea of glinting notions.

❖

When I think 'think tank' I think
trustful students in deep sea diving schools
breathing teamwork, getting the feel
of treacherous boot-licking silt,

22

and that ungilled walk, slow as solemnity,
among so many preconscious tons
pressing on that inch of rational glass;
                              getting the feel
of a slow ascent so as to decompress
such huge unfathomable density
into—some day perhaps—the sovereign
treasure of one new idea.
                              I try not to think
of all the so-to-speak think tanks:
aquariums cloudy with slogan-poop
and their hula hooping seals
as disinterested, yeah, as the tobacco lobby.

❖

"Think, pig!" as Pozzo orders Lucky
in Beckett's *Waiting for Godot*.
This command lives on in sampler form
quaintly hand stitched by my wife
and saccharinely framed (sweet,
you understand, to go with sour text).

So I bethink me.

              Could I, should I offer
a Thought-for-Today that would not add
to the world's burden of pious twaddle?
One comes to mind that thoughtful pigs,
think tanks, fore and after thoughts
might all, just for today, agree on:
              If you ever get in touch
                  with your inner onion
                      do not peel it.

WHATEVER IMAGINATION SPEAKS

Whatever imagination speaks of things
can be brought about. There will be
time warp travel, sentient robots, deep sea cities

but millions of computers in full jamboree
cannot do the math for even a few filaments
"agitating between my life and another's"

In the shimmer of web-unravelling tanglements
great demiurge imagination can go blind,
fail to look words right to their proper outcome

threads snap in a blunder of vision unaligned
with what in tangly fact is brought about:
equality stutters, utters inequality

cooperation and inclusion come out as
competition, exclusion—with sleight of rhyme
covering the slide of demiurge's diction

justice, mispronounced, joins the social climb,
lets slip her blindfold, tips a wink to privilege.
If imagination's eye and tongue go untutored

human web-work parts, drifts off into sacrilege:
light-fast trips to hell, courtesies drowned deep,
robots simulating for us all our feelings
and imagination speaking us, too, as things

AUTUMN

This must be the place:
couturier Autumn
setting styles for Fall;
I'm not a buyer really but I like to watch
his models breeze through the ritual
of their shortening days. Such theatre!
> *Pardon? ah yes,*
> *I have my invitation*
> *on me somewhere*
Such carriage! they say the secret
is in having a trapeze for pelvis
and knowing what to do with elbows
The dress tartan see-through
in green and russet is fetching
and myself, I have no problem
with that topless look—I mean,
the dimmer's on—but all the same
I'll sit here by the exit in case
some saints come marching in
> *What d'you mean,*
> *cover charge?*
uncover charge more like
this is striptease by god
not fashion
> it's chilly here, I wish
I could remember where that exit is
Autumn's gone?
you must be kidding—listen,
nobody's brought back my change
this is nothing but a clipjoint: he's parleyed
all that greenery to a fortune in gold leaf
and taken off. The thieving twit—
after this no evergreen will let me near her.
What will come between me and winter's cold?

WINTER

To think I came here by choice.
So much for free will.

Milton, it seems, was prophesying Canada:
music in hell, perhaps, but certainly the ice

One dropout from the north of heaven
must actually have liked these frozen outskirts
and after some by-lawing and sharp zonery
exercised an option to develop

He must have also been poetical,
a wordsmith of conmanship and presence
(what Aegean colleague, what Orpheus
could possibly have sawn this tundra
with his song and mesmerised the blocks
 into a Saskatoon? or strummed to life
 a body with Winnipeg, I ask you, for a navel?)
I can just hear him, wooing
our home-to-be and native land:
"Sweetums", he coughs, "your tits are Jaspers,
veritable Selkirks. Milk and honey be damned—
you will flow with oil and ski runs,
we'll make sweet CBC together."

Hopeless Dante prophesied us too,
                        had us cold:
right at the centre of our gravity
where down is up, loin deep in ice
we chew up single mothers
shit War Measures Acts
and wipe the corporate bum
with tax breaks in two languages

Saint Paul was right—
faith and hope are not enough
        Some rags of love, then, to come
between me and the winter's cold

Love believes all things
        if I can believe this place
        I can love anything
Love hopes all things
        to hope against the evidence
        is perhaps to be in love
Love endures all things—
        all right, I think
        I love you Canada

All the same, I wonder,
between sneezes, about...
I mean, *before* the fall:
How did The People hoard the sun?
What spells bound him in their pelts?

MARCH ASSIZES 2004

do you, so help you God, swear
to tell the truth, the whole truth
and nothing but the truth?
                                 what
a preposterous notion, nevertheless
I do
        in all solemnity swear
before Kofi Annan, the assembled
nations, and the League of Kyoto
Watchers, that there has been
no outbreak of global warming
in Southern Ontario for the last
five months
                 so help me God
before I perish utterly

SPRING

Last week the sun uncurled
like Jonah in the gut of winter

this week a burp of weather
fetched him up bilious
in the windows of Queens Park
where he sits rehearsing denunciations:
    Such treachery of wind!
    Asphalt crazed with salt!
    Toronto blows its nose in Lake Ontario!
The crowd loves it
chapped roads break into gap-toothed grins
twigs thaw their chilblains out with clapping

Unmoved, morose
as a too early robin
I think   Why isn't he on about Montreal
        for crapping in the St Lawrence?

Warming to his theme
he makes a pulpit of King Edward
prophesies heat to the bland pigeonry
exhorts me to repent of slush
        mend my ways of fog
        forswear the flu

but how to trust a preacher
who winters on the Riviera
polishes his rhetoric in Florida?

SUMMER

i

Black flies guard the gate of summer
all their buckyballs hysterical
with greed at how good I smell
       Did somebody mention
"spray-on lotions"?—appetizers merely
       Did someone suggest
"smear-on potions"?—so many *hors-d'oeuvres*;
proffer a lost leader, say an earlobe
or a knuckle, and blackflies will sink
a quick well on their way to drill
a whole field of leg

ii

c.f. *The Dictionary of Canadian English:*

            Summer /ˈsʌmə(r)/ *n. & v.*
—*n.***3** in Ontario the season when migrant worker
ladybugs on a recently deregulated equal payment
billing plan sling hammocks for the black fly population,
which thereupon falls into a mode of inebriated aesti-
vation (*US* **estivation**) roughly coterminous with the
months of July and August

iii

Once safely into summer—(having paid
the black fly blood-tax)—among termagant
blue jays, some muffler-challenged dirt bikes,
smog alerts, and the occasional mosquito
come singing for her supper,
there are pleasures to be had *viz*:
Sleeping naked as an egg. A porcupine
pushing its right-of-way along. Tires
whispering all those secrets to wet asphalt.

30

Watching Fran's march-past of flowers, each
unfurling its flag in due time and order.
Beer, not megacorporate gnat's piss, cold.
Crickets stuck in their balalaika groove.
        Or sun spilling florins down my back
while every cell sweats to pack its gold;
my whole body is a map of buried treasure—
if some Customs officer unzips me
the price of bullion will drop through the floor,
the Beaver Valley will be awash in nuggets
and Kimberley will outrush pale Klondike

                    iv
I have traded the stink of road rage
for the rustle of beech leaves
        I am learning the uses of something
that probably resembles happiness
        I daydream into a contented scene
Giotto-like, both solid and a-tingle:
a fresco in some angel's attic—rank on rank
of creatures, hosanna'd plenitude
including, no doubt, two rows of black flies
fluting madly on their bloodsucking straws
and a blissed out choir of cottage robbers
lip-synching *Et in Arcadia ego*…Ah well,
it's summer and I pronounce
these three acres of it peaceable

WILD TORONTO

City urgent with wildlife
concrete prairies
asphalt masticating fields
every reeking exhaust of urbanity
notwithstanding

Cardinal, local muezzin,
calls for ecumenical devotions
at first light
                I swing my creaky
gate of bones to let in day
while groundlings wait
beneath our bird feeder
for scattered breakfast largesse
from grackles,
messiest of eaters
                if this were
a fairy tale the first squirrel
to solve that feeder would have
my daughter's hand in marriage

Logging their frequent flier points
bees of various persuasions
crowd around tall thistles
beacon-blue
                Crows not only
compete with blue jays
for the town crier franchise,
they are also devoted
to warnings, early or otherwise:
they will plot you, *fortissimo*,
a fox, or some notorious cat's route

through alleyways and backyard cantons
in *contrappunto* to ants'
unnerving quietude—
so much silence from so much
busyness, absent echoes
of a million footfalls, air
palpable with telepathy

As to avian civics, I am
unreconstructedly patrician:
sparrows, I say, are noisy—
base, common, and popular;
they pose as indomitable street urchins
but they're oafs of a feather
whose waistcoats are never quite clean
                  I denounce
them—let them be set down
as no friends of chickadees

I announce I am averse
to sharing supper with wasps,
artists of unsafe lane changes
        Anyone would think I live
in a vespiary

Sometimes I wish (there goes
dove—yes she's forgotten to oil
her shoulder-blades again)
that all this urban wildlife
would just ask, then lift my latch
and move politely through my hours
        but I might as well be a set
of stop signs for all the notice
they take of me

After a bath two robins settle
into versicle and response
of contented vespers

Before long racoons will conduct
their usual moon-up debate
on the condition of our grapes

                       I swing
my creaky gate of bones
to let in night
            a subtle blend
of incense—basil, mint, oregano—
wavers in the evening air

you are of course never yourself
                              gertrude stein

They say one way of putting God
 is "The One who's uttering,
simultaneously, every possible word
past, current, or to come"—which
dignifies linguistics but encourages
garrulity in students of divinity
                    That hand-me-down
"Centre everywhere, circumference nowhere"
wears well, suggesting theological emancipation
from undue homage to that self-absorption
which so easily mutates from centred self
(beloved of gurus) to dead centre—
mortally equivocal for egos walled in
apart from any living centre's where
                              My circumference
remains distinctly undivine and local—
though it ranges wider on electronic wings
than any frigate bird—but my centre
multiplies auspiciously
                              Consider:
does not the very ability to say, "I meet myself
here there and everywhere"—adumbrate
Trinity in the very rhythm of it?
When I ask, "Who says I meet myself?",
who's speaking? When I reply, "Who's asking?"
who is it that speaks?
                              Then of course
we all know about not feeling myself today

I have mnemonic genes for reconstructing
earlier versions of myself long after

their scaffolding of cells has been sloughed off
                              and I can
think possible, even probable selves
but relations among my now-selves
prove ad hoc, somewhat tenuous, oblique

So Stein was right.
She was also very together.
So (dare we ask?) whence and what
was *her* required centripetal minimum?
God only knows.
                    Nature or nurture—
whatever is the gravity preferred for
holding my various Me's in coherent orbits—
it behoves us to keep negotiating
terms of equilibrium

Perhaps heaven is where doppelgängers
are checked in at the gates, there to fade
for want of shadow
                    and where each
improvising pronoun is transfigured,
be-nouned, proper-named, fully spoken
into a brilliant palimpsest of all itselves
and caught up in the great dance
of the centred everywhere

ORVIETO

Riding at her limestone anchors
impossible as any travel poster
                              Orvieto
basks like a fable in her harbouring fields

                    * *

Duomo, chapel of San Brizio where
Luca Signorelli's fresco demonstrates
theology's designs on shape and colour:

Riding the gale from paradise
a demon clockwork as a locust
bears a woman down through middle air

the locked fingers of their left hands
signify a whole erotics of perdition
as she looks back up at Gabriel, or Michael,
looking down on her
                          and I see
that lines of sight inscribe dimensions
of the fall, gaze of angelic brigadiers
gives true perspective on damnation
                          I see too
how I've been situated underneath
that woman in despair, how my complicit eye
became the site where composition
and exegesis draw me in:
I'm standing on the very floor of hell
it is as easy to be lost
in church as any other place,
between them Luca and his architect
have brought me to the pit, tourist
guilty of seeing, being seen

* *

Discreet dusk leaves us at a parapet
lapped by fields that ebb and glint as fireflies
hoist lanterns, fishing tremulous for love

an owl hoots once, far off, for silence
evening ponders, wise with listening trees

hoots again nearer and husky shy for lovers

again a hoot, this time close as comfort
kind Minerva's tutelary bird woos
hesitating night airs into touch with us

* *

On a crest of foothills we look back
                    Orvieto
myth of every harbour home
impossible as any travel poster
dreaming of the still white wine in her holds

FERRI DE VAUDRÉMONT RETURNING HOME
FROM THE CRUSADES, SUPPORTED BY HIS WIFE
XII century sculpture, Nancy, Chapelle des Cordeliers

Ferri de Vaudrémont
God's pilgrim-soldier, eyes too tired
to risk unfixing their hold on distances

perhaps you've just dismounted
but I think not—I see no spurs beneath
the downward press of weariness
down through long surcoat onto feet
rooted in the strangeness of an arrival
you've rehearsed a million times

returning home from the crusades
no words left—
all spent long ago: glossing vows, cursing lice,
damning all purse-lifters of the cutthroat moon,
bartering horse and other accoutrements of gentry for
dubious safe-conducts through notorious domaines,
telling your rosary of chapped furlongs
until the idea
of speech itself dropped off the end of space—
O God, that weather-raddled, month-infested space
unutterably between a sunstruck world and home

supported by his wife
whose reserve of words is also spent
to pay expenses of long absence
so, chatelaine of Vaudrémont, you just hold him—
touch alone achieves decorum of the moment,
all language else defers to enduring this return

so you just hold him
indifferent to what levantine fever,
what infidel disease might be muttering
blasphemies to his baptized marrow

I imagine him swaying but for how your arm
and slender horizontal hand, delicate
as a dove's wing-bone, share all that
vertical weight of footsore homing

   XII century sculpture, Nancy
where sometime later your Ferri lost his nose
perhaps to leprous time—who knows how
and you're not saying, just supporting him,
accepting his disfigurement as calmly
as you did that weight of weariness,
that chance of plague

Now, much later, the pair of you, patient
as your quarried genes, stand godparents
to this performance of your limestone text
about returning home

STANLEY SPENCER'S *JOHN DONNE ARRIVING IN HEAVEN*

God will speak unto me, in that voice, and
in that way, which I am most delighted with,
and most harken to. If I be covetous, God
wil tel me that heaven is a pearle, a treasure...
                                        John Donne

No cherubs, no cascading filigree
of trumpet notes, just a usual Monday
landscape in which Donne strides
in Spencer's caftan fashion
alongside Widbrook Common.
Is this earthy Giotto-solid hiker
our erstwhile Jack Donne now Dean,
our preacher-poet wired so sensually
for cerebral excitement? He looks
as if he really sees what he's looking at,
not what he's been told to see—

Stanley Spencer (age 18) insisting
that transfiguration happens
one country-lane at a time, praising
the electric ordinariness of heaven

And God will speak unto
this arriving Donne contrapuntally
in restless harmony of Senecan periods,
sonnets of angular rhythm
        and will set him down
in his roomy Cookham cottons beside Robert
Cardinal Bellarmine with instructions to relax

                    *

Which is all very well but I need
Spencer to be painting me Jerry Falwell
on some Holy Mountain lying down
with Sojourner Truth, to let me see
Pat Buchanan reach a trusting paw
into Rosemary Radford Ruether's den
or Mike Harris in Spencerian pyjamas
of plain charity eating Thai noodles
with Tommy Douglas
                     But those Falwells
Buchanans Harrises arriving in unfamiliar
heaven, their tarns of bile now glinting
sweet and deep, would be the easy part—
for how in heaven-on-earth will God
speak unto them?
               Not Dean Donne
preaching from a cloud though in none,
not Raphael, Demosthenes, Disraeli in
Committee-of-the-Whole can so much
as venture in what voice, what way
they will be greeted
               Not to fret.
I leave them to as well as in heaven
and with Spencer's vision of John Donne
in mind I practice my arrival, wondering
in what voice, in what way which I am
most delighted with and most harken to,
will God speak unto *me*?
               I be lazy—slothful even—
so might God tell me that heaven is
at least two couches, deep to perfection,
of best spanish-moroccan leather?
               (in pale green, if I'm asked)

SAINTS AND MIRACLES

Tewler has been brooding recently
about Vincent Van Gogh,
about how a painter can die poor
while one, just one of his paintings
later changes hands for sixty million
with him long gone and seeing none of it

Tewler's in *The Lowing Heifer*,
still brooding, while other regulars
deliver hop-flavoured opinions on saints
and sanctity—as good a topic as any,
observes their bartender, what with
the NHL strike and all
       Someone is allowing how
in these days of fast-tracked saints
the main qualification for beatification
seems to be become a non-stop media event
       Someone else allows how
the Chamber of Commerce is gung-ho
for saint-sponsoring, is reputed
to have said, "Saints are good for business—
they can do the serving God, we'll take care
of the serving mammon bit".
The bartender observes that maps
of her home province are crowded
with the names of bogus saints
              whereat
Tewler suddenly unbroods and after
a brief struggle with 'beatification'
joins the conversation in his two-bottle
mezzo forte voice,
           "It's the miracles.
So you don't want bogus saints?

So cut out the requirement of two
authentic miracles. Authentication
shmentication
                    every small town
hankering for its own saint has
a thriving cottage industry in miracles
and whatsifications. Cut out the miracles,
go with a life of heroic virtue—"
                    "Quite right,"
says the bartender, "much harder
to achieve—" "and much easier,"
says Tewler, "to auth…auth…to prove
                    You want a saint?
I'll give you one, Van Gogh—
a real saint, clear through to the right
to be prickly
                    You seen any of his
paintings? *Wheatfield with a Reaper*?
Starry Night? Now *there's* two
miracles for you, right?
                    But he got too far,
too close to the lava-flows of creation
and fell in. The fuses of his brain
were blown by what he most loved
and gave his life to"
                    Bemused respectful
silence greets this mix of metaphors
as a pitch for canonization
                    "I mean, in the end
he was knocked off his rocker
by the colours roaring through light
and shot himself
                    You know what?
I think despair pulled the trigger too,

despair at all that looking without seeing
which went on all around him all the time—
all those idle optic switchboards.
Wide-eyed blindness, right?
                    Anyways, it took
a saint, I say, to hang in there
as long as he did, witnessing."

WHISTLER AND MONET AT THE AGO

One in particular of these small
Whistler *Nocturnes* is burdened
with a gilt frame as grotesquely inflated
as some gouty squire's swollen foot.
It takes me a moment
to get past this frame, this gross
indelicacy, into the painting's revelation
of moonlit lagoon: What's with this yoke
of gilded wood? is it a blazonry of wealth,
some nineteenth century code for pride
of ownership?
                (My indignation has,
I fear, taken up more lines than I intended
but in fact it was, though sharp, quite brief.)

This *Nocturne* transcends its yoke
because it is a miracle laying bare
the soul of silk.
                No sanctum in Samarkand
ever had for privileged display a subtler blue
or such a bottomless smooth shimmer
of silver-grey.
                Perfection of brush
strokes has filtered out all sound:
no gnats humming Evensong,
no dogs barking even in the distance,
no garbage slurping under decaying jetties.

For having had the luck to be here,
now, in the Art Gallery of Ontario
I am granted an epiphany
of colour speaking poetry.
                Never again

can I look with pre-*Nocturne* eyes
at any body of calm night-fallen water,
faint lights on a far shore.
                              Your lily,
Whistler, still survives—no, much more
than survives—its preposterous gilding.

❖

This exhibition of course invites comparisons:
the unofficious virtuosity of Monet's surfaces
also lays secrets bare, as when he
unveils the face of Lilac within lilac;
by sheer sleight of optic accuracy
his vision also spellbinds us with
colour's fluent rhetoric of silence

but his magic can be different, too:
where Whistler's tiny piece distills
the quiet of nightfall, water, lights
to serenity entire, here Monet's
alchemical palette transmutes
unsuspecting London smog to beauty.
From the same filthy air
that coats his lungs and smarts his eyes
he sets in the zodiac of painting
a permanently auspicious alignment—
smouldering sun of unquenched red,
              Houses of Parliament,
                    river Thames.

JEAN PAUL LEMIEUX AT THE McMICHAEL

His rationed palette is like a plain
expensive ring to offset high coloured gems

Citizen Lemieux affirms, reaffirms
"*Mon pays, c'est l'hiver*", swears
allegiance in canvas after canvas;
                        Riopelle's weatherless
splendours are not for him,
our painter boreal, who could hardly wait
to return from sabbatical exile in Paris
to Québec's spacious empire of snow
where moon is pale coin in a palm of frost,
where forms like rider, coppice, train
are barely admitted inside the margins
of white seigneuries
                                    where
vizier to this sovereign luminosity
of snow is darkness:
                        black of priestly soutanes,
                        black of night skyscape—
"Moon and Clouds" with not even
a hint, really, of where the moon
might be,
                        black of "Starless Night"
where what imagined stars there are
have fallen to a chilled horizon
as pinpoints of town lights

In this country human forms—
family, neighbours, priests, Julie—
are stiff, straight-spined in corsets
of remembered cold,
foregrounded silhouettes

kept at arm's length by the scene
from rounding, deepening
into its pale vistas

In this country the palette
remains austerely minimal,
though "1910 Remembered" shows
fifty-two years of memory softening
minimal to muted
                        In its present
of 1962, "Julie and the Universe"
catches my present now-looking eye:
                        she appears
still stiff, still silhouetted, but see
how the universe has admitted her
into some elbow room from margin
toward the centre of its snowy hectares
                        see how
Lemieux's austerity has (within
winter-is-my-country decorums) relaxed
into a warmth-imagining palette
proposing the necessity of pale orange,
the absolute preciousness of red

THE STINK OF EXPERIENCE
*Let our work be so savant that it <u>seems</u>
naïve and does not stink of our experience*
Vincent van Gogh, letter to van Rappard

The energy that's gone into seeming easy
would drive a NASA fleet to Mars

Castiglione's courtier cultivated all the arts
of *sprezzatura*: appearing nonchalantly casual,
artfully artless
                and as safari leaders say
when lionesses lick their chaps and twitch
their tails, "Act natural"

How savantly, persuasively, the wondrous
gift is given of deodorants to mask
the stink of our experience

                Ah Vincent,
your orchards, skies, and starry nights, your
gala clumps and gypsy necklaces of wild flowers,
your ripe fields burning for the sickle—all may
have aspired to seem natural but they are savant
to the point of supernatural
                and those portraits—
of yourself especially—give you away:
they may seem innocent in their
bold-brushed ease but, God love you,
they stink, immortally, of our experience

Il faut imaginer Sisyphe heureaux
                              Albert Camus

What with Chatsworth Ravine
that becomes Muir Park that
becomes…etc, Yonge and Lawrence
is a good zone for minor epiphanies:

I mean, you're walking your dog
in particular October twilight
when you see in a shower
of golden leaves, round as coins,
just how easily Danaë was seduced
                              or
you're chatting with other dog-walkers—
the usual innocuous stuff—how dog shit
on pavements below the dreaming spires
of Oxford keeps things in perspective
                              or how
the Americans like to indulge every
now and then in ebullient numskulls
for President when
                              suddenly
there's this wraith of Camus saying
I'm here to remind you that my midrash
on Sisyphus does not entail belief
in some afterlife where the gods
will get you if they haven't already
                              so do not
take your death as any kind of usher,
take it as end. Full stop.
                              Reclassify
the gods, it says, *as mystifying argot*
for fantasies of post-mortem vindictiveness,

as offshore judges of mostly dubious cases—
outsourced sheriffs wild beyond any west
of justice

Make your refusal to despair the meaning
of your life and unaccomplishable toil
                                   always
you have to go on going back down
your mountain: exploit that relief for all
its worth, relish as a joy every tiny respite
blooming for dear life on your boulder

One must imagine Sisyphus as happy

                              and no,
I am not a contradiction of myself,
no evidence of any afterlife
                        I am
from deep below cobwebbed corridors
of your heart—one of your sub-basements
where you fashioned me, real as a thought,
from the red clay of my living words

AFFORDABLE WONDERS

Tewler decides that he's depleting
both savings and current accounts
of his time too quickly. He resolves
to spend less lavishly. He sees
himself being more discriminating.
I could do, he thinks, with a bit
of discernment, with some scrutability,
he says, peering into the bottom
of his teacup, where the leaves
remain as inscrutable as ever
                   though it does
come to him to spend some time, not miserly
but with due care, on wonders that are free
On mind, for instance,
which can trace inside dimensions
of its bony home, read its walls
in braille of seam, joist, contour,
with imagination's fingertips;
              which can picture
how much—emptied one day of its
unique furniture—its home is going
to resemble every other skull
now untenanted, but even so
encourages its polymathic brainchild
to signal lips for a mobile miracle of smile
at the fixed approaching grin
of vacant jaws

Or there are trees:
poplars and cottonwoods
are light-of-skirts, incorrigible flirts
who shimmy-show their underwear—

fetchingly, it must be said—
to every passing breeze
                    Whereas spruce
and firs are proper even to hauteur.
Problems of drainage are beneath them.
Their idea of a daring fling is a lacy
shawl of tamarack
                    As for pines,
they make up Ontario's presiding numen,
a trinity of pink rock, lake, and pine.
Keep still. And quiet.
You will sense reminiscences
of a time before human footfalls

Or take nightfall—
a theme known everywhere by heart
that we, of all creatures, improvise
and compose endless variations on,
such as playing it right off the scene
with lights fortissimo
              (why night*fall?* Tewler ponders,
after all, you can see night gather *rising*
in the east when sun has set)
              Like daybreak, nightfall
can usher terrors in, also worlds of wonder
of which one is that nightfall is neither
here nor there
              it refuses to be stop-
watched or kept in place by tenses
              teases us
from some kind of where between
will fall, has fallen:
elusive, magical as Pan

FABLES AND TWICE-TOLD TALES

1. THE LIMP AND THE NIGHTGALE

A certain man at certain times
      often evening, but mostly
falling between-lines-of-the-almanac times
      began to notice
that his left foot was somewhat lagging
      trust me—
a limp was pulling at leg sinister

An advice-prone nightingale perched
      on the Keatsean horn
of a now-you-see-it-now-you-don't moon
      sang *Notice that when*
you do not notice, you do not limp
      trust me—
those are the times you won't drag a foot

Asked how one keeps from noticing
the bird fell into stammers
so he shot it with his across-the-counter gun
      before blowing off
that offending too much noticed limb
      trust me—
he offed his own leg to spite his limp

He's been repaired: living nerve ends
      and fibrous silicone
spliced hands-across-the-border of his stump;
      they serve well but
things stay noticeably pins and needly
      trust me—
he often pines for the limp of his leg

2. THREE FABLES OF PLACE

all broadband calculators
for what is taking place
have been recalled by the manufacturer
as obsolete, hazardous, inimical
           to civic well being
and must be traded in NOW!
THIS MEANS YOU!
               for one (1)
virtual cockroach licensed by CRTC
to secrete the skinny on what will take place
and for one (1) transistorized bee
certified by Order-in-Council with sole
rights to manufacture what has taken place

as of noon next Tuesday
any commerce whatsoever
with what is taking place will be illegal
liable for prosecution, fine
or imprisonment or both under
the Promiscuity of Information Act

             *

It's probably not my place
to mention it, but this scene
suggests Dante taking care
of some notorious High Table crasher,
some devotee of best-seat-in-the-house
who specializes in terrifying waitresses:
        Place cards are all in mirror-
wise calligraphy so our banqueter
can try to find his place only
by looking frankly in the glass
of other eyes

56

> which leads
to such averting of his gaze
that the bill of fare's refracted
utterly to cockeyed blobs
of soup alphabetical
> A major-domo
voice piped through plastic lilies—
give place give place give place
moves him, like cilia waving
an obstruction gently, implacably
along, down
> down towards
the long table's vanishing point
where he falls off, to sit
finally beside himself
knowing his place
for ever

                    *

when I was born some god
was saying *Sorry but this place
is taken*
> Placement services
mean well but every place
they send you to is parttime
or low paying without benefits
> I live above a row
of stores in friendly sort of space
if you're OK with six a.m. deliveries
> and stairs with spooky squeaks;
I keep one bite ahead of welfare
> so, my place or yours?

of course it's a profession and yes,
streetwalking is a dangerous limbo
where all sorts of things take place
during volatile traffic in fantasies:
last week when I was down,
friend on my turf to hold my place
just made it home on all bloody fours—
but please, no let-me-cherish-you embrace,
right now all I can afford to pay is
　　　single one-way fare,
love takes capital I do not have to spare
　　　so, my place or yours?

3. REFLECTIONS

there is a certain trickster phase
of moon during which she traps reflections
in puddles, then like some loony chatelaine
dangles a key-ring of riddles
before her rain-struck victims
who mostly sink because they fail
to guess that drowning in reflections
only needs an inch
　　　　　　The odd toads
about the place were people who
guessed just close or fast enough
to as it were survive. They sit croak-wise
hoping to be cast in some TV show
where top prize is to be kissed
by a host, preferably gorgeous
　　　　　　Wavering
in the edge of these lunar reflections
The World Encyclopaedia of Fairy Tales
is ambiguous—evasive even—
about what a toad turns into, being kissed

58

4. SUBTEXT

I mean
what were those termites to think
when that Rumple-fellow's foot
came crashing through their sky?
block long disasters
of wild unmasticated wood
showering down and, for example,
flattening a whole work brigade
and three forewomen
on the ramp to Exit 37A
not to mention the ramp

humidity control was buggered up
for miles, the Dry Hack invaded
elderly thoraxes
"What", moaned
The Bugle & Borer, "will this do
to our economy?"

various Bureaus of Intelligence
offered the usual mendacities
received the usual drubbing

the Astrologist Royal was sacked—
though who cannot be crushed
by a fairy tale?
Mind you, the Brothers Grimm
got it wrong, or were delicate
about the male organ being mocked
but (as with millers' daughters)
termites entertain no such la-di-da
delicacy—their annals are crisply
unambiguous: That portent's name
was Rumpledforeskin
who will get you if you don't watch out

59

5. THE KING HER FATHER

The king her father was a major creep
who liked to watch her failed suitors bleed,
sweet she was little else than bait to serve
his bloodlust—prize perpetually withheld
to wild tunes of his orgasmic laughter.

Came the day a suitor bribed The Taster
to let the king be poisoned at his feed
with a rare dish of curried phoenix tongues,
and when his insides were all cooked and jelled
he hanged himself from a throne room rafter.

Queen and consort, they both do well enough;
their daughter grows like some exotic weed,
they long to get her throned and then retire—
now that those suitors' ghosts are all dispelled—
and live happy in the ever after.

6. IT'S IN THE SCRIPT

It's in the script
the wolf insisted,
plain as that thing you call
the nose on your face:
I get to eat both Grandma
and Red Riding Hood—
not beaten about the ears
with their umbrellas and run
out of the neighbourhood
                 he said
you can't just go changing
what's written. I'm filing
a grievance with my Local.

60

                    They said
In that case, you scruffbag,
we'll make application to have you
indicted for violence against women.
Your comeuppance will make
fun reading in "Folk Times".
                    He stood
trial (still grieving), was convicted
and duly sentenced to a stretch
in Disney films.
                    And would
you believe it children?
while out (for good behaviour)
on a holiday weekend pass
he ate a whole production crew
finishing up with the literary
consultant on a five-grain bun

7. HERE BE ELVES

I have to warn you that the elves
of Norway Bay, Québec, are tricky.

I met a man up there giving off
a faint but unmistakable odour
of post-enchantment, who said,
    There I was, trying to imitate
    the song of some bird—was it
    treet trip..cheechee bip trip or
    treep beep..cheechee pip trip?—
    when this dapper little fellow
    calls down from a branch above
    give that bird song three more tries,
    big reward if you get it right—
    I hope I'm not boring you?

No no, I said, backing off a shade.
    Good, so three tries later he tells me
    your E-sharp's off and your rhythm
    stinks. Sorry
    he says, then does a curious
    slow motion pirouette into thin air
    and hair starts growing from my insteps
    up between my toes
                  Before long
    a dapper, indeed lissom creature
    —perhaps a girl-elf—pops up
    by your dock inviting bets on how far
    selected clams will move in overnight
    toward the shore—some can make
    a good two, three feet you know—
                  Next morning
    dammit if she, it, whatever,
    doesn't pop up by the dock and say
    all bets are off! someone—you
    probably—dipped those clams
    in tincture of testosterone
    and was last seen running across
    the Ottawa river while my knuckles
    start clacking out snatches of
    Khachaturian's "Sabre Dance"
                  he says, fading
into a curious slow motion pirouette

It's later. Next thing I know that same
odour of post-enchantment chap
is looking at me across or maybe
through the hedge
    listen, he says, *I'm trying to get*
    backing for a carnival or circus act—
    hard sell, because some dapper fink

with a lissom side-kick
keeps badmouthing me to agents
                            No offense
but you don't happen to run an agency,
or have a spot of free venture capital?
                            I proffered
a toonie, my only free spot
of capital and off he went
paddling a translucent kayak…
in no time at all the only evidence
there's anything out there is my
sun-twinkled toonie bobbing off
down Quyon way

It's later. Half awake under pines
the size of Cyclops' cabers
I start tuning in a ravishing bird-call:
        listen, O my, listen! does it go
treet trip..cheechee bip trip or
treep beep..cheechee pip trip?

8. AESOP AND THE HIPPOS

A delegation of hippos
waits upon Mr Aesop, now retired,
who asks, "And what can I do for you today?"

The spokeshippo makes a leg, replying,
"We know and say you are the most admired
of all fabulists under Apollo's sway,

but permit us, as admirers,
to note with regret you've not been inspired
to set down a word about us to this day."

"Dear river-horses," he replies,
"there's rack on rack of hippo lore—required
reading about your tribe—in detailed array."

"No doubt, but we are not *storied*.
We are too big, too wondrous to be mired
in however good a natural science display;

only a story could be true
to our truth and girth. So might you be hired,
please, to fable us with minimum delay?"

Aesop replies, "Though past my best,
not open to commission, and near expired,
I'll attempt to make you storied right away.
                    Gather round:
"A delegation of hippos
waits upon Mr Aesop, now retired,
who asks, 'And what can I do for you today?...'""

~MORAL~
[Ed. note: Missing from sole surviving MS]

FOUNDING NARRATIVES

Mostly with wry disappointment
or hint of rue, people often say
"the story of my life"
                              The clue
to if they're researching their
founding narratives is usually
a matter of intonation—
with accent on the *the*
                              If you are
a serious sleuth by all means
take up life-writing—and remembering
how selective memory is, how
inventive, how addicted to deletion—
go through the door marked THIS WAY

                    Soft lore has it
that someplace on or in the door
are etched coordinates, complete
with map, bearings, destination:
notoriously cryptic but famously reliable
                    Firmer lore has it
that map, bearings, destination are
visible only to the pure in heart
so don't waste time, just go on through
and turn left at your choice of traffic lights

Don't just stand there. Sleuth

If stuck, you might want to look up
Quilto, ombuds and patron saint
of Foundation Stories
                    Do not
take offence at being addressed as

"my dear chap" or "my dear gal"—that is
as far as Quilto's come; he used
to say 'my good man' or 'dear lady'

Provided you can deflect
him from rambling on about being
some sort of nephew to the Muse
of History, he will tell you that your
rights to your own foundation story
are moot
It is the *own*,
the *own*ership, that's ambiguous because
your founding narrative is always
already part of some other author's
previous story—which frustrates
no end the tribe of copyrightniks
and assorted self-maders

He will tell you
that collective allegiance to a founding
narrative with agreed arbitrary origins
is powerfully cohesive and
invested in a mythic fiction
is also, often,
a site of lethal interpretations
and pretext for exterminations

He will tell you that every story unfolds
towards its preface ("as the Bard so aptly put it,
dear chap, 'What's past is prologue'")
He will say
"write your 'own' preface last, avoiding
the temptation to describe what follows
since what follows is already part
of someone else's foundation story"

                    he will definitely
warn you to beware of summarizing—
other founding narratives
are already plagiarizing yours,
so any summary by you is liable
to be being digested in other fonts
and elsewhere chapters

Edit if you must but not jealously;
your text is becoming less and less
authoritative and self-authenticating,
rumour to the contrary notwithstanding

That's what Quilto will say

So go back through that door
(it will still be marked THIS WAY)
and seriously get on with writing
towards your preface

AMONG BRUCKNER FANS

Things sound and smell, certainly,
as London Thameside should
in the 1590s or thereabouts
and a voice is telling Tewler to
'ware cutpurses pox and Lent police

Southwark Cathedral & Docklands
Branch of the Anton Bruckner Society
is more or less in session and
these hens for sure are veterans
of assertiveness training seminars:
a rooster's third call to order
brings only good natured abuse—
　　　　Your ideas of order are absurd
don't be such a wordy turdy-bird...

...as I was saying, Bruckner has
those horns, always those horns
sounding in thickets on the edge
of unpredictable teutonic forests...

Responses to the rooster's fourth call
to order have become quite hostile
　　　　　　Fuck off
Finger Lickin, before the Colonel gets you...

...as I was trying to say,
OK so Bruckner carves his signature
in the bark of every passage but he
doesn't moon and never swoons. Neo-
Baroque is what he is...
　　　　　　Besides,
it's such a pregnant signature—
unique que-que

Tewler ventures,
"If this is 1590's London, how come
Bruckner"—
                    Avaunt vile standing tuck
there's no need to have a bird
try not to be such a turdy nerd...
          ***I'd** like to say, love that Bruckner!*
he can drive a flock of sturdy motifs
across motley uplands without once
breaking into some damn alpine tourist tune—
                    *and **I** am here*
to tell you Denise Levertov had old A.B.
all wrapped up:
          Angel with heavy wings
          weathering the stormwracked air,
          listing heavenward
                              "Excuse me,"
Tewler offers, "but Levertov's dates"—

          Get yourself a life mister,
dreaming is as dreaming does

Someone rows up to a bankside dock,
now suspiciously resembling
Toronto Islands Ferry Terminal,
and gets Tewler to sign for a singing
telegram that commits a fugue on
Why associate Bruckner with Tudor fowl?
                    "Oafish," clucks Tewler,
"silliest question I ever heard—
who's being such a nerdy turd?
Free country, free association.
Anyway how am I supposed to know,
since dreaming is as waking does?
Or is it waking is as dreaming does?"

TADOUSSAC

Today humpbacks are doing
some seriously low feeding
or deep hold-your-breath yoga,
maybe both, indifferent to rain
tiptoeing across their sliding roof,
indifferent to the sonar pulse
of tourist wishes
                    but keeping
something of its damp bargain
with our tour boat operators
the St Lawrence flashes two, three
beluga grins, white as a saint's tooth,
between wind-wrinkled lips

Later, deep-pleated Laurentides
of Saguenay doff their misty caps
with measured courtesy of old tenants
one by one to returning seigneur sun

IDES OF FEBRUARY IN EDMONTON

Mist frozen overnight on trees
styles them in crystalline coiffure,
glittery tiaras like new duchesses

Pines in their green furs trimmed
with ermine snow are jealous
as Cinderella's sisters—no need to be:

the price of such dazzle is standing
perished in barest shirts of bark, while roots
drowsing in their dens below the frost line

know that it is not yet time to
turn on the taps or start sending up
this year's designs for spring finery

Already a pale late-rising sun is
awake enough to set about unclasping
glints of ice like discarded earrings

but these trees have had their moment—
rare, fabulous as cicada wings and
(though diaphanously brief) as real,

as authentic an entry in God's exercise
book of Things-to-Do as any diamond
in the dark waiting to be come across,
cut, and switched on by the light of day

NOCTURNE: SHANDONG CAMELOT

In this Shandong dusk
open manslaughter and
bold bawdrye aren't even in it

detached from adult mayhems,
the boy is just keeping vigil
over his adolescent love

beside his altar of a bush he offers
galahad-ridden vows, wordlessly
sincere, shapeless as Avalon mists

while she, forbidden as Guinevere
behind pale dormitory casements,
is innocent of his devotion

whenever fate grants him to meet her
she matter-of-facts him, unrequitingly
oblivious to proffered homage

Lacking the relief of seeing himself
as mooncalf, he is pressed to stillness
by his weight of yearning

in the day's last light arthurian
topography falls effortless on hills
beyond his corner of the compound wall

then in settled dark the ghost
of Malory clucks in grim sympathy:
applied chivalry is for later

PELICAN AT CAYO SANTA MARIA

Pelican drops straight down its plumb-line
onto red snapper whose improvisations
of fluid architecture are summarily accomplished
in a first and final junction: plummet and swerve,
stern perpendicular and Gaudi fluencies.

The watching tourist pleasantly full
of, among other things, red snapper,
notes pelican's lunch—the transfer
of salt buoyancy from fish to bird and
thinks:
   There's nature for you, red
in beak and fin, in fork and neat bones
at the platter's edge.
Thinks:
   just enjoy. That's nature for you too—
gratitude for clean moist-tinctured air.
Be spellbound. Listen to the Prospero sea
telling you all the secret names of turquoise.
Shed. Play footsie with this tow-head beach.
Thinks:
   these fishing pelicans at first
reminded me of Stukas—that's how
much war contaminates imagination.
Thinks:
   I'm indentured hopelessly to thinking.
I am a hub of contradictions turning
in the slow wheel of a Cuban sun,
a circus act preposterous as waxed mustachios
with my stripe-and-sabre inconsistencies
fidgeting, snarling on their stools—I wonder
which one will jump first?
Thinks:
   Let's keep our mind on pelicans,

shall we? Look at it, the only bird
that works the wind with rucksack for a chin.

So it made an end of red snapper.
Like you did.
And did those fish make a good end?
Yes. Elemental, my dear Watson—
ends without end
as long as paradise stays on hold.

So snuggle into your conflicted pleasures,
lunching pelicans included, while you may

NILE RHYTHMS

They're still a good way off,
sound and sight in syncopated rhythm:

up front, facing rowers, drummer beats
     as oars sweep
    dig and pull
    dig and pull
on the prow sits singer, facing forwards
singing charts for voyage homeward:
currents, rest-stops, shoals,
     at the last
a leaning jetty, women waiting
    dig and pull
    dig and pull

They're much closer now,
sound and sight in rhythmic synchrony:

drum is rocking rowers on their seats
    dig and pull
    dig and pull
tune-compassed singer casts a line
of song, reels the future in towards
     tilt and swish of boat
    dig and pull
    dig and pull
at the last a leaning jetty, women waiting

TRAVEL/LOG

When I said to the man at a bar
in Cochrane that I don't do hunting,
I could see him
         registering me
as a suspiciously humanoid form of life
on the loose from the deeps, maybe,
of the Greater Toronto Area
         sizing me up
as a possible trophy for his rec room wall

        *

My shoes have this thing for water
mysterious as a masonic ritual
         Consider:
on a mission to pay homage
at Dostoievski's grave I'm standing
in a square of truly soviet dimensions
         the weather's fine
it hasn't rained for days, no fountains
no sprinklers, a babushka sweeping
bone dry cobblestones
when Fran is suddenly mirthful—
my right shoe has found a tiny puddle
the only water as far as eye can see

maybe I should just give in
and head for Venice

        *

Some places more than others
are given to palimpsest: In Rome
there is a preserved bit of archaeological dig
tidily shored up and glazed over;

76

                    I peer down
past cross-sections of history
to the Appian Way, which lets my gaze through it
till I can make out—not quite erased by the tramp
of legions—Plato and Aristotle thinking
immortal thoughts on the backs of slaves.
My gaze focuses back up
to the rectangle of ancient Roman road:
maybe these very pavement stones
centuries beneath my feet were close
to where the heart of heaving Spartacus
gave its last despairing thump

My day long foot-tour of Rome finishes
with supper in a recommended *taverna*
where vino loosens my tongue enough
for me to try telling the owner
that I am visiting from Florence—
Ah Firenze! piccola ma bella!—
the best Italian, he avers, is spoken
by a florentine tongue in a roman mouth
(or was it the other way round?)
and my halting attempt to locate
the most beautiful Italian I'd yet heard
in the mouth of a museum guard in Lucca
was not, I could see, entirely convincing

On the way back to my *pensione* I think
an unChamber-of-Commerce thought:
                    by now surely
some economic historian must have
calculated the value of slave labour
to the GNP of ancient Rome.

In bed I review
the marvellous urban archive
I was walking through today
                    I still see, though,
between its lines the ghosts of slaves
mouthing their erased names and words

WHEN TEWLER SINGS BLUES

    When Tewler sings blues
they can be robin egg with just a hint—
a remembered echo—of yearning
for some pulse of spring
                    or
they might be turquoise with just a tint
of summer sweetness undercoating
                    melancholy

    When Tewler sings blues
sometimes they're indigo with just a glint
of violet to give edge-softening
shape to sorrow
                    but
cobalt is his signature blueprint—
pure unplagiarized sadness distilling
                    almost a joy

SONG

that wraps up memories
   in rare expensive silk
that charms hurt hearts to bloom
   deep red again with trust
sing me such a song
    such a song

that lifts a roister cup
   pick-me-up for passion
that makes a bedding room
   smirk in sheet-wrinkled lust
sing me such a song
    such a song

that beckons me to sup
   again with absent pleasures
that ambushes my gloom
   with laughter fit to bust
sing me such a song
    such a song

WORD OF THE HEDGEHOG

I sing in the stone choir
of the west façade's great portal,
Amiens cathedral.
                         Actually, I hum.

Unlike that bird in the chiselled alcove
just above me—still full of curiosity
alert and unabashed after 800 years—
I bow a modest head among
the grand and royal harmonies
of my portal.
                         Here I am, low slung
witness to the inclusive exuberance
of a master mason's creative plenitude:
                         hoisted
out of under-a-hedgerow anonymity
to be a sign, celebration too, of worship
also being in the details.

                         To every condition
its temptations: I must admit that,
humming along in pink warm light
of some late summer sunset, sometimes
I feel quite proud of my humility;
but under the correction of January sleet
I recover the creaturely humility
not to be outraged by outrageous weathers.

WORD OF THE JUNCO

Here I am, set down diminutive
but palpable in black and white.

It would take a senior lawyer
to misconstrue me
                    To announce
"I signify therefore I am" is a bit
pretentious in such a small fellow,
maybe "I am therefore I signify"
would be more socially acceptable
but in all modesty I have to say
I am a whole micro-signifying system:
as in, sign of sartorial elegance among
the upper class and penguins, as in
sign of harmonious race relations—
white and black in edenesque accord.
        I am icon of the black and white (ah
the deep deceptiveness of its simplicity)
so beloved of the best photographers
        I wear my formals every day
my body lives easy in them
unlike some whose bodies inhabit
their tuxedos about as fluently
as Dorothy's tin guy in the Wiz of Oz
        You should see my tiny seed-exposing
tap-dance on the snow—as neat
and economical as Pierre Trudeau's
pirouette behind the Queen
                            Rigged
as smartly as a great house butler
but also casual cool and, let's face it,
so succinctly packaged. That's me.
Welcome to dapperdom

WORD OF THE STONE

My rigidity of skin
does not limit my sphere
of influence all that much

for instance, softness and I
understand each other very well
for I am mattress to quilts
and contours of the world

You want fashion?—
eat your heart out Madonna, Gaia
has been wearing me interchangeably
as over and underwear for years

I am president of the Republic of Weight
though in moments of slingshot lightness
I have knocked off giants.
I have been tattooed with covenants.
I am Uluru, hub round which Australia wheels

Speaking of sacred places—
I both make and mark

WORD OF THE SWALLOW

Though I entertain residual doubts
about a straight line being
the shortest distance between two points,
geometry is easy
and generally reliable.
      At dusk I sky-write
new chapters on the art
of navigation instant and precise
      What do you want to know
about arcs and tangents?
the homeward bisection of an angle?
About improvising circumferences,
dare-devilling sudden curves?
      Did I mention tangents?
They aren't just something you go off on,
above water they are plunging lines of approach
towards the lightest microsecond of a kiss
      I am tailor to the Queen of Light;
all day, with scissory swoops,
I crazy quilt the air for her.
      I am the next move
in the dance of flying insects:
they whisper in my gullet, "Yes,
I will oil your Euclidean gyroscope for you."

MERCY JONES SUITE

[1]
A BALLAD OF MERCY JONES

Her fortune cookie said:
Stay well away from all left-footed crows.
Beware of maggots squirming in the truth.
Avoid all uncracked Edwardian mirrors.
Take care: a lot of middle aged badgers
will snip belly buttons off for worry beads.
And never go up to the attic early—
      so it goes and so it goes
      but her heart beats burly

Her *Who's Who* entry said:
a club-foot rooster diced her two big toes,
phantom transactions ached away her tooth,
her eye rolled wrong way through a one-way glass,
a wombat raising funds for Sydney zoo
set her nipple in a ring for his true love,
she went up to the attic much too early—
      so it goes and so it goes
      but her heart beats burly

As far as God alone can tell
she outfits moulting birds in furbelows
and keeps her CEO dolls bibbed and couth
and leans through shiny surfaces with care
and rigs doorbells with fur-trade balance sheets
should the beaver she was sweet on once call by
and still she climbs up to the attic early—
      so it goes and so it goes
      but her heart beats burly

MERCY JONES GOES TO TWILLINGATE

"Away from home the general idea,"
      says Mercy Jones
as a born-again fishing boat trawls her,
damp as a tourist, through an excursion
"is to be skilled as your own look-alike
for dear only knows the sort you might meet
and home was never, not ever like this."

"I fancy these icebergs for my totem,"
      says Mercy Jones
as a brace of cod-forsaken seiners
curtsey to the guillimot-waving wind
"I'd love to move *my* weight so quietlike
and of all creatures they alone sweat sweet,
no, home was never, not ever like this."

"Sun's been taken sudden with blurred vision,"
      says Mercy Jones
as wheelhouse shelves rattle their popcan teeth
and fog-doused Crow Head bellowing *Stand off!*
"so maybe I shouldn't have hitched this hike
so where is the land to set my two feet?
oh home was never, not ever like this."

"Bless fog come and gone, bless the humpbacked sea,"
      says Mercy Jones
as she makes ceremonious drying out
with warm scones, partridgeberry jam, and tea
"bless Kettle Cove terns in hover and strike
bless pitcher plants tiptoeing on peat
ah home was never, not ever like this."

MERCY JONES REVIEWS HER LOVE LIFE

I swore by all
the sixty names of snow
I would be true to him.
He said, I don't really know,
you have some blue ice in your eye
and anyway I'd prefer you slimmer.
Will he come to love me soon? I ask
the seven-veiled Northern Lights of
my summer heat-wave dreams, who reply
Sometimes yes, sometimes no

I swore by all
sixty-three names of sand
I would love none but her.
She said, I don't understand
that X-ray gleam of candour in your eye
besides, you've got a nipple missing.
Do you think she loves me yet? I ask
the bare-legged siren palm trees of
my winter cold-snap dreams, who reply
Don't ask, our music's canned

I swore by the whole
lexicon of private parts
I'd be their lusty love.
They said, In our heart of hearts
we're blistered by that oven in your eye
besides, you never wash our underwear.
Will they be faithful to me? I ask
my first editions of *Pillow
Talk* and *The Joy of Sex*, who reply
Perhaps—in fits and start

This winter finds me unattached
my own company excepted
(with which, I must say, I'm quite taken).
Bread, wine, pine logs are all hithered,
toasty buttered, mulled, and neatly stacked
To Bach's *Christmas Oratorio*
I gingerly unwrap an unexpected gift
that has the feel of contentedness.
No carrying on soap-operatically,
no abandoned ballad-wench, no forsaken
devotee of *True Romance* withered
of all hopeful fantasy.
                    Cheers!
my knickers aren't in any knot,
at year's end I like me quite a lot

[4]
MERCY JONES SINGS IN THE BATHTUB

It's true I'm missing some small body parts
lost here and there to trophy-hunting arts.
I gave police a full check-list
but they have only time enough
for serious expensive stuff
> *sing me sober, sing me pissed,*
> *one goes on—you get my gist?*

In pawnshops where I hope to come across
what's gone, they mostly say, Write off your loss.
I know that love's a risky gift
to be accepted gingerly
but the wrappings always get me
> *sing me cheery, sing me miffed,*
> *one goes on—you get my drift?*

Always is a good time to be kissed
no way I'm going to offer then resist.
Though not entirely ship-shapely
I am more than most can handle
burning both ends of my candle
> *sing me taken, sing me free*
> *one goes on—you follow me?*

MERCY JONES DECIDES SHE'S NOT
YET READY FOR THE SHELF

Yes a man I lived with once
left me for the other woman
who turned out to be a man
    but that didn't bother me
    well, not all that much

Yes my importance dwindles
it's not escaped my notice
that day, my friends, and all things
    are less apt to stay for me
    I can't blame them much

Yes my degrading thirst for
outrageous stimulation
seems to be in jeopardy
    which to tell true bothers me
    though not terribly much

Yes my boombox larynx has
lost power, but troglodytes
still call me strident feminist
    and shrill—which reassures me
    rather more than much

[6]
MERCY JONES REMEMBERS
THAT IT'S THURSDAY

...Wednesday's child is full of woe,
Thursday's child has far to go...

I've seen the back of forty-nine,
the back of forty-nine is scaly
rather too much like a dragon
             I should know
whose tail lashed me into fifty
whether I ducked quick or slow
I still had far to go, far to go

I edged cautious past fifty-nine,
the haunt of that age is a bridge
where fifty-nine, flea-bitten troll,
             I should know
scrabbed and scratched me into sixty
whether I jumped quick or slow
still I had far to go, far to go

I dip and rock to sixty-nine
in paper boats and pension cheques
sixty-nine's a dolled up siren
             I should know
crooning rumours about seventy
whether I sail by quick or slow
there might be far to go, far to go

the road inclines, the sun is out
that haze ahead is seventy-nine
if I find Time hiding there
         I'll let you know
meanwhile grandsons skateboard about
I kind of like the status quo
could there be far to go, far to go?

90

**MERCY JONES CONSIDERS
WRITING HER MEMOIRS**

If I presume to set my memoirs down
they'll best be prefaced by my epitaph:
I made life speak me in an exotic tongue,
made even my coldest presiding stars
        waltz stiffly to my roaring

An early morning in late May squeezes
me, tight as pip from lemon, into life;
oceanic bliss is vacuumed from each lung
and after a pipe-cleaning cough or two
        I lose no time in roaring

On second thought that's all the time I'll spend
on memoirs—I'm too taken up with now.
All those moments that slipped me as I clung!
Memory's too sedate an editor—I intend
        to get on with my roaring

BAG LADY

She never begs, don't ask when last she ate.
Who knows what Sophie stashes in those bags?
Her Day-Glo button says Let's party late.

Her wobbly pram's packed heavier than fate
but, pushing her Long March, she never flags
and never begs, don't ask when last she ate.

Such nook-lore, connoisseur of the warm grate,
doyenne of evaded loitering tags,
her Day-Glo button says Let's party late.

Does she carry some howling inner freight
all this baggage both signifies and gags?
She never begs, don't ask when last she ate.

Greet if you must, do not commiserate—
her eyes will hoist red scorn like battle flags
though Day-Glo button says Let's party late.

She is a touch uncanny in her gait,
might she be Wisdom harlequin'd in rags?
She never begs, don't ask when last she ate,
her Day-Glo button says Let's party late.

WE REFUSE

Colt revolver
called 'Peacemaker
and/or 'Widow Maker'
cult-ridden fetish—
why do so many men
so venerate inflicted death?—
icon, essence of macho
law and ordering: fake
solutions by real violence
        Colonies of ants
forget their migraines
their sky of dusty pavement
for once is not throbbing
with helicopters is not
leaking bloody slogans
        Whole orchestras
of crickets stop to listen
to this huge quiet of absent
tank-treads, battlecrying
funerals
        There are women
moving in this silence
Israeli, Palestinian
Jewish, Muslim
courageous as a trunkful
of Victoria Crosses
they are holding hands
under a banner WE REFUSE
TO BE ENEMIES
        Be careful,
gentlemen, to pretend
they are not there,
take care not to honour

their armistice—after all
you have your ancient tradition
of fake solutions by real violence
to uphold
                    these women
pacing out their dusty peace
refusing to be enemies
could be dangerous

GLIMPSES

In this season of pliant loyalties
and debased rhetoric of heroism,
let us now praise actual heroes, like
women fiercely loyal to being human,
'witty of themselves'—with it
in a big way and persistently
courageous, in for the long haul

DOLORES CACUANGO helps lead
the Ecuadorian Federation of Indians,
founds four indigenous bilingual
schools in the 1930s
                    hacking at
obstacles with her machete of a will,
she breaks through to a glimpse
of bliss:
            pupils crying for joy to see
on the page, hear in the steaming air
how their native Kichwa enters
its full dignity of trading meaning
sign for sign, sound for sound,
even with the conqueror's Spanish

ASIYE ZEBEK. In Turkey to be editor
of an independent magazine, one is
already edging close to heroism

As female editor of an independent
magazine one is certifiably heroic
and if the journal is of socialist persuasion

one's already in the pantheon of heroes.
The half-expected knock on Asiye Zebek's door
comes in 1997, she being all of twenty-six

and about to spend the next five years
of her life—being raped repeatedly—
in prison with no suggestion of a trial

The sight of one jailhouse vermin
or another violating what little reeking
space she tries to cling to, and unbuttoning

its trousers, must be a glimpse of the abyss.
More, more glimpses recede like replicating
mirror images into a vista-without-end

of the deepest halls of hell.
                                    I lay
on those jailhouse vermin, those mange-
ridden jackals they call masters, this curse—

it delivers her no justice, brings no doom
down on them, serving only in an act
of frail solidarity to vent my feelings—

I tell you, churlish Turks, Asiye Zebek
will be a ministering angel when you
lie howling
                    She is a pearl

in the lowest sewer of state-terrorism
while above ground, apparatchiks perfume
the nation's armpits to go wooing the E.U.

Shine, Asiye, and fare well
                              but avoid
Canada—our otherwise risible security
apparatus knows all about oppressing

the already oppressed, all about holding
people indefinitely without trial while
perfuming its armpits to go wooing the U.S.
which, in this lethal farce, is serenading Turkey

AUNG SAN SUU KYI turns 63, June 2008

How does this woman stay so calm,
so serene, this winner still in waiting,
while the likes of Pinochet and his merry band
of Disappearists, or those Greek colonels
and all those other ghosts of tinpot juntas
mock her from the shadowy slums of history?

How long, O Lord? Is there no balm
in Myanmar? Those generals, sating
themselves on a cowed, supine land—
can she unplug them? interrupt their knells
over elections? cancel their death-cell quotas?
uncover their plunder in full inventory?

96

Her rare freed words sing like a psalm
of sanity. Those pigs in uniform grating
on freedom's nerves occasionally slip up and
we briefly hear her voice of liberty that quells
their grunting law-and-order mantras,
and glimpse in her a democratic herstory.

FREEDOM CIRCA 2001-2008

we are gathered grieving here
to mourn the death of *Freedom*,
lovely among words upon the tongue
       Freedom: as words go
more abused than most, mispronounced,
brave sound more than most pried loose
and untimely ripped from the embrace
of what she signifies
            Now, alas, mac-
cheney'd, bushwhacked:
               mantra'd into
an abstract wraith shorn of incarnate
prepositions—her niceties of 'to', her
locomotive 'from', raped to the hum
of Washington and Jefferson spinning
in their insulted graves,
               plucked to dress up
imperial satraps as tutors in democracy
and left for dead in the gold-dust of
contractors stampeding to Iraq

But friends, let us stay in resurrection mode.
With new vaccines brewing against Manifest Destiny
Freedom's unknuckled consonants will re-knit,
refusing to be loaded dice in White House crap-shoots
            Her sprung vowels
will hear the U.S. genius for decency clear
its throat and re-collect themselves, stooping
to their proper perch in the civil lexicon
           She will again
keep watch, fierce-eyed, on the wrist
of what she signifies

LITURGY

From his pulpit of stock options
he waves auditors' reports creative
as the first six days of Genesis
        shouting
Blessed are the risk takers
for their profits shall rise like incense
glory glory to the Bottom Line!
  Where have all the pensions gone?
  Way down in Enron land

The surest way to defend
civil liberties is to abridge them
it shortens the defence perimeter
        he cries
Blessed are the interrogators
for they shall see truth naked
glory glory to the Bottom Line!
  Where have the detainees gone?
  Way down in Gitmo land

Citizens at large are not stake-holders
never miss a chance to privatize
O friends! taxes are so evil, evil
        sobbing
Blessed are those who hunger
        and thirst after loopholes
for they shall be filled with rebates
glory glory to the Bottom Line!
  Where have all the clean streets gone?
  Way down in gated land

There are no deserving poor
welfare makes laziness, gnaws the spine
of competition and free enterprise
             shouting
Blessed are the speculators
for they shall hold entire nations to ransom
glory glory to the Bottom Line!
   Where have the sea otters gone?
   Way down in Exxon land

MEMO TO LORD ACTON

so does powerlessness
        not mention
absolute powerlessness

ROVING REPORTER

1

Good morning, Canada, this rover-report
comes to you from a phone booth on the corner
of Dundas West and Ossington. About 6 o'clock
this A.M. on my walk-and-jog, I pulled a fistful
of Texan buckshot out of two whooping cranes
cunningly disguised as Minister of Justice
and Citizenship & Immigration. By way of thanks
they told me where to find Osama bin Laden.
I e-mailed the White House with an offer
to sell this information, but Dubya was busy
with cosmetic enhancement of the space
between his eyes and replied, "Call again
when your cute dollar is down to 60 cents US."

2

Good evening, Canada, this rover-report
is coming to you from 42nd Street where—
good god!—the Digital Newspeak Synthesizer
has just broken down—*hey this is big! big! where
are you Peter Mansbridge when we need you?*—
and the famous twinklies of Times Square are
reporting news in real English. My camerawoman
has been arrested for smoking Cuban cigars
in a public place, but I can read you what the lights
are spelling out:
      THE ONLY PARADE IN TOWN THESE DAYS
IS A LONE FOUR-BLOCK FLOAT FEATURING A SIX STOREY EAGLE.
SNUGGLED BETWEEN ITS THREE METER TALONS IS A REPLICA—

...ATTENDED BY COMPUTER-GENERATED MODELS OF DEVOUT
THREE AND FOUR STAR GENERALS—OF THE SHRINE DEEP
IN THE RECESSES OF WASHINGTON D.C.'S SMALL COLON...

...WHERE, PRAYER SHAWLS EMBROIDERED WITH
THE NUCLEAR OPTION AND KNEELING ON THEIR COMFY
SUNDAY WAR MAPS ORIENTED EAST, ZEALOTS OF EVERY SECT—

...DEFENCE, CIA, JUSTICE, PNAC—LATELY IN MORTAL DANGER
OF RUNNING OUT OF ENEMIES, GIVE ECUMENICAL THANKS
FOR THE SADDAM HUSSEINS OF THIS WORLD...

...BEVIES OF MRS CLEANS CARTWHEEL BACK AND FORTH
ALONG THE FLOAT, THEIR RED WHITE AND BLUE
DESIGNER PANTIES SPELLING OUT FOR VIEWERS OVERSEAS...

...*YOU TOO CAN JOIN THE AXIS OF EVIL! HELP KEEP THE WAR
ON TERROR GOING!* THE SMELL IS COMING FROM BENEATH
THE FLOAT WHERE, NAKED BEHIND A SCREEN OF FLAGS...

...THOUSANDS OF DETAINEES, PRE-SHRUNK FOR EASIER
RACIAL PROFILING, PEDAL DESPERATELY. THEY'VE BEEN
STRIP SEARCHED (FOR WHO KNOWS WHICH ORIFICE...

...A MINIATURIZED WMD MIGHT BE UP OR IN?) AND
POSSES OF MEDIA HAVE ESCORTED THEIR CIVIL RIGHTS
TO THE CLEANERS. FRESHENING UP THE STREETS...

...AFTER THE A-TEAM'S PARADE ARE B-TEAM—LET'S HEAR IT
FOR BRITISH BLAIR!—AND C-TEAM, LET'S KINDA HEAR IT
FOR CANADIAN CHRÉTIEN, WHO'S PASSING (MORE OR LESS)...

...ON IRAQ BUT BIDDING ON AFGHANISTAN. THEY BOW
AND SCRAPE, LIMBER AS ACROBATS. JEAN'S SCRAPE COULD DO
WITH POLISHING, TONY'S BOW IS SUAVE AS SAVILLE ROW...

...AFTER THE—

Um. Sorry about the interruption folks, a CSIS
power-action doll has just rappelled down my shirt
and shot the mike out of my hand. I'll return you
to CBC Newsroom then try to find my thumb.

                    3
Good afternoon, Canada. I am rover-reporting
this bracing autumn day from Arizona, most recent
stop on my post-thumb convalescent odyssey.

102

I have to tell you, America is *very* beautiful.
But first, thank you for all the cards: 52% Get Well,
31% Get Stuffed, 8.5% Thumbs Up, 6% Undecided,
and 2.5% randomly impounded for an anthrax check

My camerawoman is OK. She was released
into the custody of the Fraser Institute
and reprogrammed in its basement to think
Jamaican and Dutch cigarillos only. For saving
Canada-US relations the CSIS power-action doll
was awarded a microdot Order of Canada and promoted
to paperweight in the Solicitor-General's out-tray.

Back to my convalescent odyssey: Shaky start.
US Immigration was disinclined to let me in
but when I translated to their satisfaction
the *Dieu et mon Droit* tattooed on my latex thumb,
and pointed out that my god-rest-it real thumb
had died for freedom of speech on American soil,
they broke down and waved me through in tears.

As I was saying, America can be very beautiful.
In Arizona I'm in the middle, hardly believing,
of what must be God's own sculpture garden.
New Mexico is Georgia O'Keeffe beautiful.
I swear the last hamadryads sigh in the pines
of Oregon. Think New England's autumn quilt;
think mist rising over the Alleghenies.

Rosa Parks, Fannie Lou Hamer, you are beautiful.
Judge Welsh, unflappably irradiating the cancer
of McCarthyism, you and all the noble race
of US whistleblowers are beautiful—you too, Anita,
diddled by the Senate Old Boy club, which was
only to be expected, but to hear some black sisters
call you uppity cut even a white-ass male like me.

Adrienne Rich, Audre Lorde yes, Richard Wilbur,
Gwendolyn Brooks, Wendell Berry, Marilyn
Hacker, yes beautiful. Language will rise up
in the mouth of later poets to call you blessed.
Blues, mistress of the ceremonies of yearning,
Muhammad Ali, splendid black orchid
blooming over boxing's dung heap, you are—

Excuse me…one moment please….My producer
is frothing into his mike. I am to cut the maudlin
elitist crap (his words). I've just told him to eff off—
I'm in my groove of celebrating what's to celebrate
in the US of A and barely started.
                              He's just fired me.
I shall retire up to Mohawk Nation territory and give
seminars on keeping borders permeable. Ciao.

SETTLERS

Eden was the only founding settlement
not to displace settlers originally there

Such pristine occupation, non invasive,
innocent, is not recoverable

every occupation since then
is a dispute among squatters or
an invasion with dogmas for precedent,
articles of faith for title, technology
and brute force as sole arbiters

Since then all paradises
are emblems of desire deferred;
every apocalypse that unleashes
a thunder-clapping Judgement Day
is sign of justice postponed, denied

Listen: As you move through your present
playing whatever lyre fate dealt you,
you must believe, oh steadfastly, that
your origins are right there behind you,
but turn to face them, pull them to you,
and they will fade scolding, like Eurydice

Listen: With your despair of origins,
your true believing in whatever Promised Land
with God as your very own indulgent landlord—
you, I say *all* of you, are the true idolaters:
it is your own fierce longing that you worship

Do not settle. Sojourn—before unpeopled Earth
proclaims silently that no one owned any of her

DIPTYCH IN *THE TORONTO STAR*

DATELINE WEDNESDAY 12 SEPTEMBER 2001
FORLORN HOPE
RACHEL UCHITEL MAKES AN EMOTIONAL PLEA FOR
INFORMATION ABOUT HER FIANCÉ, JAMES ANDREW
O'GRADY, OUTSIDE BELLEVUE HOSPITAL CENTER IN
MANHATTAN. O'GRADY HAD BEEN WORKING ON THE
104TH FLOOR OF 2 WORLD TRADE CENTER WHEN THE
THE PLANES HIT.

> Trying to look
> I try not to look—
> should any human eye
> flinching in shamed modesty
> before this naked agony
> be privy to such pain?
>   a sight,
> even by electronic proxy,
> to scorch the retina:
> Rachel weeping for her man

DATELINE WEDNESDAY 12 SEPTEMBER 2001
HOME DESTROYED
ASHIA ABU NAB WEEPS AS SHE SITS ATOP THE RUBBLE
OF HER HOME, DEMOLISHED BY ISRAELI FORCES, IN
EAST JERUSALEM. THE ARMY ENCIRCLED JENIN
UNDER COVER OF DARKNESS YESTERDAY.

> Shrieks of 200 years
> of olive tree being ripped out
> still razoring her eardrums
> she sits on bulldozed leftovers—
> terrible garbage of macho politics,
> of being absolutely eye-for-eye
> *Gott-mit-uns* right—

                    arms spread
        in Eve's first despairing semaphore:
        Ashia weeping for her home

Sir:
I remember wondering why
the newsprint did not curl burning
in my hand
                    I remember being
grateful for every technology from
language itself on down that showed me
while shielding me from such agony,
such despair
                    And believe it
or not, there are still people
who walk this earth unable
to connect the crucifixions
of Rachel Uchitel and Ashia Abu Nab

PROMISED LAND

You protest the imagery
                 theology
                 geography
                 & politics
are wrong. The myth won't work.
How could God have been so careless
with the script—even in fun—you say,
as to let those colonizers
so far mistake their part for Joshua's?

But casting was exact,
the adaption impeccable:
for Hivites
                 read Beothuk
for Jebusites and Perizzites
                 read Plains Cree and Haida
for Canaanites
                 read Huron

(some, inept with sources,
mere allegorists,
have been known to read
for Amorites the Québecois)

Myth is alive and well in us
chers lecteurs and *semblables*

it is very hard to edit
for a happy ending

LOOKING BACK

They might perhaps have been forewarned
about blood on the leopard's paw,
fish stuffed in pelican billfolds,
clove-scented unicorns unhorned,
fruit gone strange, so sudden prickly;
but looking disenchanted back
at Eden what they thought they saw
was that warm oh soft lap hardening quickly
under newly intemperate heats and colds

They might have been enough suborned
by hints of mastery red-raw,
of booty and palatial strongholds
to have abandoned it unmourned—
God's green word still flowering thickly—
but at the last turn of the track
from Eden what they thought they saw
was that warm oh soft breast fade in sickly
rags of scarecrow dusk where some dark thing scolds

TIME/S TABLE

Time is the mercy of eternity, which permits us—
sometimes and only for a time—to parse it
into our lives' sentence, hoping to trap it
in a net of rhetoric and grammar.
> *At the gate of Eden Eve*
> *trips over a foundling, she calls it Time* 1

We tell time who, uncircumspect, will tell.
Time offers us some chiastic exchanges—
passes time/time passes—but does not often
indulge such affable reciprocities
> *Never an easy child, Time*
> *ignores curfews and stays out to all hours* 2

We serve time, do time, try to pass time who,
bad driver, won't move over into the slow lane;
but we also buy, save, spend, waste, even make time:
zany economics of surplus scarcities
> *Time's out-of-wedlock daughter,*
> *Truth, keeps trying to sue for child support* 3

Efforts to find, have, take, keep time notwithstanding,
it's usually up—never takes itself down for a nap.
Time might let us try lacking, losing, calling,
marking, redeeming it, but mostly it just flies
> *Time bungee-jumps into west,*
> *rebounds behind us with east-dampened hair* 4

Wherever some fading mind has flickered out
a syllable among the names for time is lost
so, since to live up to its names time lives on us,
it's anxious to bring women to their time
> *As age nudges us downstream*
> *Time tries teaching us illicit backstrokes* 5

110

When we've all disappeared into pluperfect
time will re-submerge, anonymous again,
in currents of unconjugated tenses
bearing along all noises but the sound of speech
        On their Ancient Classics dig
        angels find bones that might be spelling 'Time' 6

1 time was we were an interesting adaption
2 time was we were a promising experiment
3 time was we were a *comme ci, comme ça* adventure
4 time was we were a dangerous development
5 time was we were a lethal auto-mutation
6 'Time' (as it were) will still be; we will have been

PILGRIM'S PROGRESS

The idea of trumpets sounding
for him on the other side sounded
good to him. So he set off.

At the passport office
they said *Take a number*
have a seat while we look you up
in Kafka's **Castle**.
                    Some months
later when he asserted rights
of being noticed, this innocent
joke went round the office
like a viagra-addled flea. *His rights!*
O la! listen to the lad creaked
a supervisor, tears of laughter
glinting on her mandibles. *Take*
a number, have a seat while
we consult the interdepartmental
Torah on **Through the Looking-Glass**
                    *

At the visa office they said
No, no, not that *green card*
which notwithstanding and/or
in any case has been maxed out
by our agents camped behind
your mum's china cabinet
                    we need
authorization, sworn and witnessed,
for such fellows as you to be crawling
between earth and heaven.
                    *

At the Ministry of Health
he asked—by way of the *Freedom*

112

of Information Act—for a prognosis.
You still owe, they said,
*for the procedure that separated
your I from your Me.*
    *But if you admit
to being human, confess mortality
and sign here, we can tell you what
is* not *in store for you:*
    *Roses will
never sheath their swords for you,
the stirrup moon will not hoist you
up to any wishing star*
     *

Close to Citizenship & Immigration
two scurvy parrots parted him
from his last fiver—the one
exhorting him to row, row, row
your fucking boat, the other
to take it easy, surf the ether, dude,
surf the ether
    *Anything
to declare?* Customs asked,
*moral bankruptcy? undying love?
psittacosis?* He declared himself
a missing person which amused
Customs no end. They plied him
with impounded brandy, playing
their genial truncheons
about his ankles
    Who'd miss you?
they said *you have to have
somewhere to be missing from*
they said *now get lost
so **we** can declare you missing*
     *

At the border post
they said *See over there? Hell*
and Heaven both lie yonder,
equally virtual and chiefly
crowd control devices. So unless
you're addicted to Sweet Certainty
do not go that way
                    But he did.
When he pushed into her dressing room
in hopes of surprising her
with daffodils and dew-minted heather,
he fouled his pants in terror
and stumbled stinking out
for Sweet Certainty was lounging
in a wrap of human skins and the face
she turned to him was blank
as any locust's
                    *

So here we are they said
half dead under a vision-tree
in this mother of all nowheres—
your moment, as the saying goes,
of truth.
              Earth's armies have all clanked by,
every one in firm cahoots with God
                              He cried
Oh I am wicked! wicked!
                    They did
a Google search of the ***Inferno***
but he was nowhere to be found
                    The romance
of grand sins, said the Red Queen
sharply, *is much overrated*

                    *

They say he struggled
as far as some delicate beach
beside a playful, dangerous sea.
They say he puffed into a conch
with his last breath
                    mumbling
that he could hear an echo
of distant trumpets
                    Pish and shush
they said as they laid him out
for burial
                    Note, however,
that every long-prepared obituary,
now dusted off, was fulsome;
that the good he did was not interred
with his bones and certainly
lives after him. It took six
motorcycle cops to massage
his cortège along.
His requiem service was packed
to the last usher
                    And though yes,
they sounded for him on *this* side
the hosanna trumpets
in Bach's *Mass in B Minor* were
without clapped out exaggeration
heavenly

ORNITHOLOGY 101

The doctor-Livingstone-I-presume of birds,
albatross ply everywhere currents
to ends of earth, huge sails proclaiming
the gospel of unlocked from land

but sometimes one rides
its archangelic span of wing
into peril's range—its true north seduced
perhaps by iron in the crossbow bolt—
and for all its seven-seas buoyancy
is abruptly martyred as a trophy
hanging from some freebooter's neck
                    whose stupid mouth
can explain no better than *there was*
a set-free beauty in its life
that made mine ugly as a prison

in the dead ensuing calm
joys of sunshine innocently
concoct a stench of gratuitous death

two thousand kilometres away
in a passion of wind
a young albatross has memorized
its catechism for trusting unfolded wings;
it flops and flaps towards
total immersion in baptismal air,
unlocked from land

∽

As falcons go I am
a peregrine of descent

as fine-feathered as any bird could wish.
The Ark of Noah, *flottante*, is in
our coat of arms, sign of the Great Ordeal.
Have you ever had to perch for months
neb by rump with your natural born dinner
of *Columbidae* peasantry and never
so much as twitch a talon in their direction?
one's DNA still damn near
unhelixes itself at the mere echo of the thought
of such tormented discipline, but
falco peregrinus chivalry endured
austere, impeccable—even extending
a courteous head start to pigeonry
and doves on disembarkation day

We are big in our avian firmament:
one pair in our ancestral pedigree met,
served—and woo'd—in Chaucer's Parliament
of Fowls, speaking up shrewd and raptorly
          In many a fine lady's
Book of Hours we graced a wrist,
stooped to lure, or seized on game;
our hooded dreams were wild
though we seemed tame
          Our roll of civic
and battle honours is book length
          We were icons,
heraldic birds of feudal field and castle
Now we keep democratic office hours.
I was born and raised on a downtown ledge,
urban pigeons are my prey
          My last one,
a Sunday strike, I ate between Eaton Centre
and Church of the Holy Trinity's south door.

I hope the scriptured folk
who watched me dine read, marked, learned
and inwardly digested that lesson
from God's other book.

᭡

Sparrows form that class of bird
which puts the gristle
in words like *jostle bustle*

Sparrows should be, if they are not,
on every syllabus of Electrical Engineering
since with no discernible effort
they adapt to all known voltages
of place and weather.
                    If they are not,
they should be in every Baedeker
for space explorers, since sparrows
will already be there, wherever,
free-for-alling local pecking orders
and touting pre-surveyed, pre-serviced
feeding stations.

᭡

In my Hotel Caserio room
Playa del Inglès, Gran Canaria
I wake up to someone whistling

sun-swigging Brits
have taught the hotel parrot
the first few bars of "Colonel Bogey"

118

maybe those notes evoke a memory
in some cellar of its parrot genes
of being an extra in *Bridge*
on the River Kwai

                              but if so,
most of that jaunty dirge
for so many casualties
has been walled up
in some yet deeper cellar,
for despite patient poolside tutoring
by guests (myself included)
I waken every morning

                              waiting...
but that second shoe—
the next few bars of "Colonel Bogey"—
never drops

SERVING A SUMMONS ON MEMORY

In the night Tewler's dream-gerbil
climbs into its wheel and sets off
on the anxious run towards
a familiar non-arrival:
                         Typically
he is late and while time fidgets
delays seep into the scene:

He hurries up and down wrong platforms.
Which pocket was his passport in?
Affable passers-by, cruelly calm,
give directions that take him through
abandoned factories to some warehouse door
that opens onto a vanishing point of *déjà vu*.
He knows his somewhere audience
is melting through the exits
while he fumbles for a set of notes.

As usual, the very moment these frustrations
run out of time some gatekeeper snores
loud enough for him to segue into waking.

Sometimes he drops off again,
sometimes, just drifting, he ponders:
I must be programmed to like plans
that turn out as planned;
I've been invested in order—especially
its modes predictable and punctual.

More or less awake, he asks, Where
does this dream come from?
                    If memory serves

He is seven, going on eight,
they're doing the Trans-Siberian railway
Hard Class—fixed wooden benches
and bring your-own blankets.
At every station, even before the train
has groaned to a stop, his father
joins the rush towards the lone standpipe
which, he's learned, is more august,
more precious than all twelve
pearly gates of New Jerusalem
in his Children's Illustrated Bible.
He doesn't dare leave the bottom step
of the carriage for fear the train
moves off without him—
though the heart-squeezing weight
of his anxiety should be enough
to weld it to the rails.
That standpipe queue isn't getting shorter
will Dad have time to fill the kettle?
will that piddly flow of water peter out?
what if, oh what if the train
***does** leave him behind, stranded*
in a vast siberia of non-arrival?

His father never did get left behind
with that kettle—dinted grail
of sacramental drinking water—
priceless as the casque of Galahad
in Tewler's copy of *King Arthur and His Knights*.
Though he has recovered *that* saga's
manic roller-coaster of anxieties and reliefs,
gerbil-dreamwork does recur. He suspects
his memory of withholding full disclosure.
        Meanwhile there is another day
to face down, or up to.

OUT: THEME AND VARIATIONS

1. PRINTOUT FROM DOWN UNDER

Inland from the Sunshine Coast
look out for people on the lookout
for lookouts, they're over fond
of heights, given to braking suddenly
at the prospect of a prospect and
their outlook on life tends to be
a camcorder window
                whereas sudden
braking is rarely problematical
in the outback, where proximities
are outsourced to sweatshop horizons
and red-carpet space keeps unrolling
outbound towards some ceremony
of arrival at postponed outskirts

2. DIRGE FOR A POEM UNFOUND

Sometimes OUT		sometimes OUT		
takes precedence:		will follow on:		
there are		as in		
outages	outboards	back out	beat out	
outcasts	outcrops	or (you get		
outdoors	outfields	the picture)		
outfitters	outflows	black		bliss
outgrowths	outhouses	blow		break
outlanders	outlaws	brown		butt
outlooks	outposts	fall		farm
outriders		flame		flip
not to mention		flood		fold
out-of-towners		fork	&	freak

122

OUT can out and out precede and follow itself. As a minor deity in the pantheon of words OUT is a Janus guy who faces both ways:

> break{out}break
> lay{out}lay
> look{out}look
> put{out}put
> run{out}run
> sell{out}sell
> stay{out}stay

Somewhere in such linguistic fecundities there must be a poem, perhaps even a found poem. But the muse is OUT

3. *PETITION TO THE* **SOCIETY FOR THE RECOVERY OF MISSING PREFIXIVE ANTONYMS** *ON BEHALF OF* **CITIZENS FOR DECENT FLEXIBILITIES IN ENGLISH CANADIAN USAGE**

In the matter of the word OUT~
we your humble petitioners, the better
to curb the headlong, indiscriminate,
lewd couplings of the said word OUT,
do herewith respectfully pray SRMPA~
to install, promote, & otherwise confer
lexical legitimacy & currency upon
       INRAGE
& we respectfully crave leave~
to serve notice upon SRMPA
that CDFECU is at this present
engaged in duly member-authorized
debate on the merits of conferring
lexical legitimacy & currency upon

INWIT   INFOX   INSMART
as verbs of the transitive persuasion❦
       We remain,
Yours in a spirit of inrageousness,
              CDFECU

   4. *FREE-STANDING OUTS*

Remember to tread warily around
free-standing Outs detached from
obligations and dependencies among
branching sentences of words

Always such Outs arrogate
to themselves degrees of authority,
even if they rest upon benign usages
of conventional consent
                 as when
umpires call "Out!" in swift arbitration
between competing hopes—those cheers
and groans, happy uproars and mute glooms
which orchestrate the lonely walk
back to bench, dugout or pavilion

Sometimes such conventional
authority stretches to include
discipline, as when the exasperated
teacher's "Out!" ends in a bench-vigil
next to the office of Vice-Principal
                or even reach
to discretionary use of force, as when
the bouncer's "Out!" puts period
to the truculence of some drunk patron.

124

Definitely beware the imperial Out
affecting to be autochthonic, if not
self-created; it spurns the family tree
of syntax, carrying on as if all its meaning
were in itself alone
                              Sometimes
such imperial authority parses into
micro-despotisms—c.f. Victorian fathers
who, in melancholy novels, banish
fallen daughters: "Out!" they bellow—
or worse, whisper through clenched teeth—
and with that imperious syllable cleave
all grammars of affinity and familiar
constructions of home and hearth

Beware and resist, resist betimes
the viral Out that, cultured in slogans,
infects whole populations to make fodder
of themselves for dictatorship,
spiritual and/or secular
                              as when "Out!"
bled Moors from Spain's body politic,
leaving racist tyranny roaring religiously
in a savaged garden where once grew
Arab astronomy, engineering, medicine,
mathematics, and philosophy
                              as when
a million Jewish ears began ringing
to the sound of "Out!" "Out!" "Out!"
until, much worse, unimaginably
worse, those Outs mutated into millions more
of insults and privations, into forced labour,
into ghettoes and starvation, into death squads,
into the final acrid silence of smoke
drifting over ovens

125

IT

You know the twinkling
of bicycle wheel spokes
in a summer sun?
         Well **it**
can be as innocent as that,
especially when climbing into bed
with that hospitable verb **to be**
and hatching **S**'s: *it's a fine day*
             it's all right
             it's an elegant solution
But **to be** is of notoriously
easy virtue and keeps getting
it into all kinds of trouble—
I mean, what if "it's a fine day
for blasting steel through moose
with Remington Specials?" Or if
"it's all right, Mr Cortez sir, you go to it,
they're only unchristened savages"?
Or if "it's only a knee-cap—
next time pay up on schedule"?
What price now, that offspring **S**? her
lissom innocence taken advantage of
by **to be's** unscrupulous boyfriends?

Worse is the **it** unmoored, drifting
past every familiar wharf of nouns,
leaking open to inrush of terror and despair
             it's in the air
             it's snuffling outside the tent
             it's coming closer
like stealth bombers, ghosts
with pale spines harder than titanium
             it's just the way things are
             it's all up, finished

126

But worst—worse than imaginary footfalls
coming true in moon-abandoned parking lots
are all species of the bumphoid **it**
with their slave traffic in tortured passives
(may their toothless gums be gnawed forever
in the deeps of hell, O Lord, by hard clean prose)
> *it's been decided*
> *it's been brought to our attention*
By whom? Who? we ask, disconsolate as owls
that cruise the edge of once dear copses
clear cut now, no longer rustling
with the small precisions of a living **it**.

NUANCES

on the patio of *The Lowing Heifer*
        Tewler is into a second half-pint
of Skeena Wolfgang's—second half-pints
        are his preferred mode of rocking
between nostalgia and regret

though by the end of that second glass
        regret has usually seeped into elegy
            Lately he's been
on about creeping devaluations
        in the currency of words. Nuances,
he says, it's about eroding the stock
        of available nuances

        Oh he knows
that language is a life-form fabulous,
        protean, whose meanings can mutate
on the very tongue that's speaking them
        and now he's grieving for *disinterested*

disinterested, he mourns, is disappearing
        down the gullet of *uninterested*,
there goes another nuance, dammit,
        that debases *interest* while they're at it

        Oh he smiles
in lugubrious agreement when his friends
        tease him about all this fretting

        Oh he knows
that letters to the editor, rearguard actions
        in some classroom, pontifications
of Academies, French and otherwise,

are hopes as forlorn as the 'Last Post'
but as member of a signifying species
        he feels duty-bound to say words
over endangered and vanished meaning,
                so he ups
and declaims (though not so as to strain
        decorums of *The Lowing Heifer's* patio):

                        for want
of a nuance the sentence flounders
                        for want
of a sentence the paragraph sinks
                        for want
of a paragraph the communiqué implodes
                        for want
of a communiqué the whole effing conference
        falls apart at its recriminating seams,
a tremor quivers through the magic castle
        of meaning, causing yet another fissure
in its uttermost basement where grunts, squeals,
        howls of proto-speech are still housed

keep the faith with your nuances,
        says Tewler to the waitress
on his way out, and keep the change

SANTA PASSES TIME ON THE CORNER
OF YONGE AND ADELAIDE

Only
7 more shopping days
        doing our bit for late capitalism:
        this is your Commercial Only

passports
non-smokers   only
ticket holders
        answering the passion to sort:
        this is your Taxonomical Only

exit
entrance   only
one way
        going orderly with the flow:
        this is your Directional Only

men
whites   only
members
        excluding constitutes inclusion:
        this is your Patriarchal Only

three drops
with meals   only
for external use
        intimating our mortality:
        this is your Pharmaceutical Only

and no doubt   Pragmatical
                Fantastical
                Puritanical

Casuistical
Hierarchical
Problematical
maybe even
Hermeneutical
Onlys

only when I look passers-by in the eye
when only I look passers-by in the eye
when I only look passers-by in the eye
when I look only passers-by in the eye
when I look passers-by only in the eye

only a stupid word game: I was only kidding: only 33
minutes 11 seconds left in this shift: the one and only:
only if: if only I could go back to the beginning: only until:
only after certain conditions: only when &/or if circum-
stances permit: I'm not only kidding: only 27 minutes even:
simulation only, simulation only: only in cases of extreme

ohhhnnleee!

you heard me, so listen up: soundwise,
only is only an L away from lonely
you get the picture: all the others
have fallen down the pockets of their santa-suits
only I, I only have escaped to tell you

STABAT MATER

Lady of Sorrows
seven more thorns
to sew on your wimple
seven more griefs
to pluck at your heartstrings

          one is
the sweet green moment of a bush
gone forever, charred and stonied
to prone trunks and branches ages down
where memory's blind miner digs for warmth
the ash-bound cold black chunks of time

          two is
the hunt for certainty—that ridiculous safari
sweating along after man-eating truth
but only ever stumbling on its slogan spoor
and
vultures picking bones of last week's certitude
and
crepuscular hyenas yakking jokes
about reality being hazardous to health

          three is
Eve and her Adam stripped naked
of unknowing as they thread the eye
of innocence to darn their skirts of leaf,
          but Lady Mother,
grieve for the serpent too—
touching an astounded tongue
along his length of banishment, incredulous
to hear his eloquence construed as heresy

132

four is
all hot gospellers
who knock their well-tuned heads together
and like the absoluteness of the ringing pitch,
who use the tread of dynasties as pocket metronomes
and sell hellfire insurance by the heavenful
with latest jingles about Armageddon;
they sing out the commands that fire off
scripture's multipurpose canon, that keep God
practicing right turn on their parade square,
presenting arms to their well woven flag of texts

five is
the flabbergasted tars on Breughel's ship
who comradely jump overboard to fish
for bits of Icarus to save up for the decent urn,
but seeing him drowned and happy at the last
among cool fish, they turn to be hauled in
and set down sputtering on the salt familiar deck.
Then in their warming cups they say: Pity—
but it serves him bloody right for flying high,
the other one stayed low and look,
he's made it to the coast

six is
the lamb you suckled, Mother,
who grew—remember?—into a lion
who got into hell's own fight with Leviathan
and ripped his belly out.
                        But it was comfy there
gestating quietly in the dark—what contractions,
what groans of labour were there to warn us
before your ruthless midwife of a lion
pulled us out mewling in a blaze of yellow eyes?

before a file of tongue was rasping us
damn near to death? before that fiery breath
had lit our little candles for the windy world
to blow? before a monstrous paw
had started cuffing glory into us?

              seven is
skull as concentration camp:
              where I wait
behind barking slogans under
the searching light of towered eyes,
for an amnesty of unclenched hands or
the miracle of a foul-up acknowledged or
perhaps a raven on my window-sill
green password in its beak
              Freedom is scarce:
the going currency for bribes
remains mysterious, tunnels collapse,
ink on my only map of outside is
implacably invisible
              They say that
the occasional escapers
who tunnel past their own entanglements
soon learn those strollers blessedly outside
are inmates of other compounds—
the usual suspects—accused,
like oneself, of god knows what,
and also dreaming, maybe, of ravens
with green passwords in their beaks
              It seems, Lady,
that very few of all the rumoured breakouts
will see a meeting of free fugitives

MOTHER AND CHILD: BESLAN

You crouch, hand soft
as a yearning feather
brushing your child's forehead

your touch could be tenderest
of goodnight blessings
                          except that
it is full day, pitiless—shameless
to be lighting such a scene

it could be most delicate
of wake-up touches
so as not to startle your child
out of sleep
                          except that
the life stunned out of her left
telltale reds of abrupt absence
about her mouth and nostrils

In this news-photo moment
one of death's paparazzi
has made an icon of you—not a *pietà*
for, though unearthly beautiful,
you are impossibly serene

every swirl and surf of grief
has for the moment ebbed
from your shock-enchanted beaches

But in the deep of you
will feelings grind and stir
into a tsunami that will tumble you
in the salt debris of your hopes

                    douse you
in surges of rage and sorrow,
rank eddies of despair, disgust
all the way to Moscow?

where you will again become
a photo-op while the President
of Mother Russia tells you—
                    you, a mother
of Beslan, all about terrorists

TEWLER DECIDES NOT TO RENOVATE

I feel time treading my floorboards—
not even bothering any more
to tiptoe—and again I wonder,
creaking, how on earth did he lay hands
on living-room, bedroom, kitchen keys?

Renovation is big these days,
pricey extreme makeovers galore;
once, I confess, I almost added
my off-true nose and sagging backside
to the approved shopping list of worries,

imagined tubes slurping cellulite—
this was during that panic uproar
over the Perfection Deficiency Syndrome.
But I've grown up. If my bum droops
I still can touch toes and see my knees.

Barely a single cosmetic cut
can claim necessity: suctions or
remodellings, lifts or body sculptings
are hard to make a virtue of, whereas
I make some virtue of no remedies.

I'm history, more cuffed around by weather,
joists on strike for better climate control.
I declare myself a Heritage Site:
summer's cottage once, now autumn lodge,
soon alpine shelter leaning against northerlies.

In this self-rehabitation mode
I'll not tinker much with my abode.

GETTING REAL ABOUT REALITY SHOWS

...all the world's a stage,
And all the men and women merely players:
They have their exits and their entrances;
And one man in his time plays many parts,...
As You Like It, Act II, Scene vii

Yes, yes, it's agreed that all the world's
a stage where, witting or not, we act out
roles: prompters, scene-fillers, bit parts,
protagonists—mundane, inflated, genuine—
buffooneries, the dark stations of Iago.

I can take direction well enough
but I am in-house director, too,
of my own performances: choreographing
gestures, timing duration of a smile,
estimating the leeway between my space
and another's.
                                One of my roles
is closet critic (let's keep this just
between ourselves—I'm uneasy
about being outed as a critic, but
stage directions for this scene call for
a dash of honesty)
                                This critic-self
is a ruthless bugger who's never
had the grace to doze off during
any of my acts. Even if I've brought
the house down he will proffer
some stinkweed of a quibble
among roses of applause;
                                if I flub,
or even worse and god forbid,
merely go through the motions...let's

just say 'implacable' isn't even close.
              In theatre bars,
where he should be stroking
my thespian egos, he carries on
about Aristotelian mimesis, mutters
scholastic distinctions about degrees
of make-believe truth-telling.

At improvisation—he lunges—
I am a total flop: a hit, I must admit,
a palpable hit; then skewers me
on a sneer about pathetic ad libbers
who have no serviceable small talk,
though I'd have thought my repertoire
of banalities about the weather
is truly impressive.
              I *am* my roles
and he forgets that he is one of them,
yet I note how quick he is to join me
on stage to bow and bask in whatever
sounds as if it might be clapping.

In defence of this outed critic-self
I suppose it could be said that he
and my director-self between them
keep me in non-stop rehearsal
for my farewell performance and final exit—
eternal Monday of my last dark day:
curtain down, two cleaning women
hoovering fugitive echoes of my voice,
bare marquee waiting in I hope, soft rain,
for letters to spell out new play, new player.

OBSEQUIES

BEATRIZ EUGENIA BARRIOS MARROQUIN
Assassinated December 1985 just before she
was leaving to fly to Canada

On that day
       you take a too late taxi and
       truth worse than any nightmare
       yourself in your own hearse
       no warrior-god in the midst
       of you and four assassins
       to keep you safe
On that day
       driving to golgotha, no song for you
       of bridegroom-god exulting
       only the beat of impotent power
                    systole
       of blood-lust, diastole of hate
On that day
       was the Holy One—any holy one—
       there in that machismo fog to meet you
             hands hacked off
             face chopped up
       death being smashed into your head?
On that day
       when you receive her
Mother, Guatemalan earth,
give her back as flowers
that wave to us like hands
that smile like the face
she used to turn toward her sons

BRIAN HEENEY
1933-1983

In one cell's delighted minuet
             suddenly
        a stumble
at first the dance resumes
his brain still setting words,
whole chapters, even, to harmony
of blood, bone, nerve
              but then
dancers   misremember steps
start dervishing up and down
his astonished corridors
             chaos
in crescendo, some wrong voice
calling the wrong tune

Where were you, Maestro Jesus?
No need for the fortissimo
that recomposed mute Lazarus,
one grace note would have done

I re-read the resurrection score
but all I really hear are dissonant
             modulations
wife to widow, child to orphan

My last sight of Brian helps:
he steps across our lawn
his body, his whole being
concentrated on the chords for walking
he moves (a slight stumble) in April light
out homeward through the park

CHARLES FEILDING
1902-1978

When you felt the stinking goaler
unlock you, body skewered
on his skeleton key and
shrieking on its rusty hinge,
and knew your patient gown
was turning to a shroud
did you, pastor, with your clear
but modest sense of an occasion
plan this one too?

   old man in a box
   who, being dead, yet lives
   who being gone, is here
   and—friendly teacher still—reminds us:
   this is the way, no loitering by graves,
   this is the truth, do not be sentimental,
   this is the life, believe me as you can

   old man in a box
   you, as always, waken charities in us
   and from the plague of all our houses
   make of us true synod—
   three hundred voices join in thanks for you
   and, full of grace, we make of this,
   your last but how perpetual occasion,
   the immemorial feast of bread and wine:
   Do this in remembrance, friends, of me

JOAN IVES-COLEMAN
1930-2001

Oyez! Look, look at a swan
calming the landscape down
and think of Joan
                    Not placid,
but moving on the waters of her life
in serene determination

Long ago pain arrived to visit you
then decided to move in for the duration
but like any real alchemist
you kept transmuting the lead
of protesting nerves and muscles into gold:
a whole emporium of accomplishments,
everything pristinely untawdry
burnished, thoughtful in its place

Your beloved Shakespeare's Richard,
second of that name, said famously,
I wasted time, and now doth time waste me.
You wasted so little time that Time found
there was nothing in you to waste away
            The best, the worst he could do
was breach one of the dykes running through
your brain's rich tulip fields and let you go.

I remember how modestly you fitted
your large talent in loose dresses,
a violet scent of wholesomeness,
straw hats of lawn-sale chic
                    But I think:
That modesty won't cut much ice in heaven.
As recent arrival, there's no use

sidling in and picking up
the smallest triangle in God's orchestra;
when you so much as tap it,
it will sound out Mozart's *Exultate, jubilate*
full volume, complete

                      Complete, dear Joan,
in the old, still proper sense: perfected

MARGARET FRAZER
1916-1985

Teacher is right

The foolishness in us
you swallowed not gladly, but
with a pinch of your tart seasoning,
gracefully enough
Lately you were reading feminists—
theology, poetry, psychology—
taking it for granted, at 68,
that you should be teaching,
still, the lesson of yourself-
as-woman to yourself
                        Then you let us
student teachers join you in your
house-school for your final term
                        Here, you said,
here is my body (it wasn't easy
letting us be pupils of your privacy)
read me, write me in your daybook,
I am the body of your text
text of your bodies;
learn yourselves in me.

You had us all to school.

By the time death stayed
overnight and did its laundry
in your lungs we were inscribed
deep in your closing chapter
and you in our continuing stories.
We are still learning, for only God
She knows how much you had to teach us.

MATTHEW DOLMAGE
Bracebridge 1974 - Toronto 2004

Not to bother rehearsing
admission speeches for St Peter;
just exchange the usual touch
of biceps and knuckle-brush of noses—
such an original rhetoric of permission
to come aboard will tickle him
no end
      And do not be forgetting
your wheelchair. You might want
to dust it off and wheel it out
now and then for old times' sake
Imagine:

      You and FDR
madly wheelchair surfing,
catching waves that keep shifting
into dolphin particles, getting up
inside the curve of some cresting
constellation as it begins
a for-the-fun-of-it plunge
into God's unfathomableness

Imagine some now-and-always day
going for a spin, improvising
jazzy music of the spheres on
the universe's bottom-deep B flat
or, simply for its own sweet sake,
setting groups of founding equations
to new harmonics of your own—
all the while playing chicken
with Time at the speed of light

NORMAN FELTES
1932-2000

Your list of terrorists—including
fear of going ga-ga and a whole
mug-shot parade of Philip Berrigan's
"well manicured barbarians
at the controls"—did not include dying

Tall aristocrat of conscience
you came to exercise such strong
preferential options for the poor
as to be accolated "traitor to his class"
at your wake in the Danforth Irish pub

Contempt for $800 suits—Lilliputians
signing giant expense accounts while
saying we must all make sacrifices—came
easy to you, connoisseur of difference
between real change and band-aids,

yet you inhabited that ironic gracious inch
beside yourself which loaned perspective
to the eye inside your eyes; you could see
yourself in round, tell stories on yourself,
even cast yourself sometimes as buffoon

so it was not some bewildered stranger
being hustled through his last extremity
of shade down into sinew-loosening surf
but you, uniquely Norman, standing
out to sea mainmast tall in farewell light

PATRICIA CORRIGAL
Ash Wednesday 1998

When I arrived holiday fresh on Sunday
to hear, Patricia, that you'd just died
the garland of my Cuban suntan
turned to ash while I searched
all my dictionaries of brain and bone
to make sense of such mortal nonsense

Sometimes the grammar of hope is too difficult,
too many irregularities, peculiar idioms
   What good did it do your blood
to flout its own syntax and drown itself
inside your skull?
   Why should friendly murmur
of your body's language stop like that?

Sometimes the grammar of hope is so difficult
but John, Isaiah—you yourself Patricia—help us now
to coin some hopeful sentence-fragments like

   Death, you are too late:
already the garland of her life is set green
among the ashes of her going. Too late: the living
waters of her faith have begun to slake our grief
   We call her an oak grown into its rightness
with roots too deep, far too intertwined with ours
for you, Death, to go uprooting

In us she's already entered the last day of her festival,
the great day, and she calls to let the good tears flow,
to drink in the memory of her—garland green
         rooted oak
         water

PRIYA SARKAR
1929-2003

However your death sounds to us—
surprising as a sudden gong,
or soft note of a vigil's end,
we hallow absence with this song:

Stars sang the ballad of your birth
when you rocked in on a red tide,
they wrapped your cries in silver tunes,
winked you to sleep, well lullabied.

In the rich echoes of your life
we hear with reverence again
the cadence of mortality,
our beat of joy, our pause of pain.

Now you have drawn your curtained eyes,
rejoined creation's larger choir
to sing your Bach, to ride God's gales,
and dance in elemental fire.

Such thoughts, such memories—they make
a complicated farewell to a complex man;
small bell, white roses, Tia reading—make
simple farewell to an unassuming man.

SALVE, JUNE
for June McMaster, d.1986

Such talent for renewal you had
for transforming clichés, so even
in the fearful outrage you felt there

in Zurich, when illiterate mortality
first openly began to edit you, you wove
new texture to the story of your life

planned further installments, insisting
that rights to your history were no easy bargain.
Then with death writing you toward closure

in the standard version, you resisted
his stock of commonplaces, plotted
not platitudes like happy ending

formulas of happily ever after,
but rarities of joy unconventionally
close to the last page. Our tired lexicon,

how much of it you energized:
for instance, *heroine*: gracious as silk,
entertaining us in your living room

while feral pain stirs in its net of drugs
and you unable not to wonder
if your day's brave weaving is to be

unravelled in the night against your will.
Later, in your dying room you struggle
to answer greetings, still heroine

152

though spun out to the last thread of thin.
Salve, June! your name on the tongue
is like a month of weddings,

go with whichever goddess loomed you
while not unhopelessly we fabricate
for real a text of memories together
to wear against the chill of absence.

SMALL SISTER
Beijing 1930 - Jinan 1936

A race's memory of loss
moves in my father's face
keening its way into a hymn

My mother heavy, pressed
to the shape of Eve's astonishment
at death
        Both dry, unable yet to taste
the gift of tears from friends

Myself the boy afraid, almost, to breathe
that air so dense with desolation, watches
their look not focussed yet into belief,
eyes still round with the deceit of it:
                        Death
dressed informally in a sore throat
dropped round and took her so politely,
so without the usual oratory of dissolution

So smooth a theft
such an easy getaway

Two Chinese gravediggers
patient with foreign rituals
wait to spread his same old soiled blanket
this time on Merle's fragile cooling bones
then leave us, resurrection far away,
to hear what comfortable words we may

THAT THIN MAN
for Eli Mandel 1922-1992

Years ago and weighty
with many words to come
Sometimes, you said,
I see myself as a thin man

That thin man hid at length
among your other doppelgängers—
which you was it hustling tickets
to your Big Top of Words   words
                    making proud grammars
roar with surprise at strange commands?
                    oompapahing high wire
acts of speech while athletic phrases
launch at each other's wrists,
never a safety net of platitudes in sight?

Nightly in dreams   shapechanger
you improvise yourselves:

spider
    ambushing yesterday's clichés
    to spin tomorrow's cobweb truth
beachcomber
    uninnocently strolling, taking
    your poems as you find them
clown
    tumbling images from an old magician's coat
    uncanny pockets inside pockets
                            inside pockets
criminal
    loitering with intent among
    fabulous women in the unexplained interior

or even (eat your heart out Proteus)
keynote speaker
    asserting in so many words that
    all assertions have as punch line an evasion

Then once upon a time a stroke
not knowing who was who
bushwhacked all of you but one,
that one among your doubles
that thin man bespoke so long ago

Whoever you were
had troubled Hades many times
to rediscover poetry and bring her singing back
               That last time, though,
your one remaining head was turned
you were sat immobile in a wheelchair
dressed in tracksuit, running shoes—
all the manuals of style
yapping in triumph
as your beloved figure of speech
faltered   receded into silence

But listen   listen

From your body's text
the body of your text's
alive with versions of you
unauthorized and authorized
       telling
             calling
uttering your magic dialect
in silent speaking words

VAL HUDSON
student & teacher d.1979

The setting Glendon
Shakespeare is the text
You introduce yourself
and we begin to improvise
our appearance in each other's script
Soon we are working out
exchange of friendly narratives:
in mine of you, you study
always to say things as they are
       I come to read you more
as colleague than my student,
fill in a character of you as one
who tries to turn truth's next corner
without cutting it
       Now your ending's
caught me by surprise, sad
in this unlooked for turn of plot
but I imagine you—blond, brown-eyed—
saying
       Don't skip this scene
       or try rewriting it;
       I told my death
       how she could have me
       and she took me up on it

By your exit my continuing roles
are diminished, seem incomplete
       You'd be impatient with obituaries
but I hope that your receding shade
hears this: You left me a better
teacher than you found me

WILLIAM COLEMAN
d. July, 1992

So generously you planted so many
trees of knowledge, landscaping
so many minds toward their kinds of Eden

how well you knew that words,
each leafy word you spoke had—
even as you spoke it—two tongues at least,

that divinely good ideas are junkbebonded
into fortunes, that rain-rich forests
are daily chain sawed into toothpick slogans

but undiscouraged, you went on planting us
in words as careful as may be, so that now, you gone,
we stretch a little toward your kind of Eden

where what you thought, said, did,
moves pungent in us, wise as sunlight
but crow-sharp and feisty as a jay

WREATH FOR THE MONTREAL 14

.i.

There are never enough flowers
and flowers are never enough

even so
a wreath for fourteen women
killed in the middle of their wish
to profess something besides...
so: amaranth, anemone for two Anne-Maries
apple blossom for Annette
amaryllis for Annie
buttercup, begonia for two Barbaras
gladiolus for Geneviève
honeysuckle for Hélène
maidenhair, marigold for two Maryses
sweet marjoram for Maud
michaelmas daisy for Michèle
nasturtium for Natalie
stonecrop for Sonia
all working, learning
to profess something besides
cunt and tits, good girlishness, wifehood,
motherhood, spinsterhood, kitchen, and
all the costumes of Girl Friday

.ii.

Fourteen women
withered from their professions
in a blast from the metallic penis
of some would-be man disabled,
trying to write off his primal debt,
unable to live with the sacred riddle
of his emergence between a woman's legs

159

and nerved, finally, to take revenge
on debt, on riddle, on his phantom Woman
by encoding independent women 'all feminists'

.iii.
Where was I when…?
                        Down under.
Montreal to Auckland another fault-line
lurches, another volcano in the gynophobic
chain erupts, spurting and drooling—
the obscenely usual cocktail. Old skin
of eyes and ears burns off in its lethal glow,
I see, I hear the song and dance of pundits
dressed in TV cabinets, national-geographic perfect
for armchair tourists:
        No no! it was just a random incident,
        one isolated nutcase; no more poison
        where that single boil came from

.iv.
this wreath of not enough flowers
I've been rolling uphill for 13 years
toward some propitiatory rite,
some hilltop altar, gets heavier
with each step up daily media reports
                        Remembering
is right, proper, unanswerably dutiful
yet attar of memory is so delicate
and not only sexist fumes or air-addling smog
but time, sour breathing time itself
curls and browns the edges of my wreath.
So here, above the tree line of my life,
I need names of flowers, wafts of memory;
I need green names of fourteen women
to help keep remembrance, hope, fury

clear and present
                   Forgive me,
Barbara, Maryse, Hélène, Maud,
Anne-Marie: any taking of your names
is bound to be in vain
                   Forgive me,
Annette, Sonia, Annie, Maryse, each
in your world-without-end singularity
for making the group of you a sign
of every woman dead by male violence
                   Forgive me,
Natalie, Geneviève, Anne-Marie, Barbara,
Michèle: every gesture of memorial
from strangers is also an expropriation

               .v.
Endless multiple orgasms of weaponry, yes;
women as sex-toys, yes of course,
or Thatchie dolls, busy about being
as dangerous as men can be, that too;
old wars obsessively revisited, oh yes,
but the ruling obsession
of our entertainment moguls
is all the possible ways a woman
can be terrorized.
               O, I have ta'en
too little care of this! I confess
I have not hoped enough, not raged enough
I confess that flowers are not enough,
that designing Women's Studies courses,
that having lots of close and trusting
women friends, that being shriven daily,
freely, by the patience of women
unknown to me is not enough
—my wits begin to turn—

                    I confess
that confession is not nearly good enough
*some*one must take down *all* the names!
they must be there and decipherable
for some judgement day
                            I say
proper notice must be, must be taken
let the record
            let the record
                    (to deal plainly,
I fear I am not in my perfect mind)

                    .vi.
modest as a dung-beetle I will go on
rolling my wreath uphill
                        do not laugh at me
for, as I am a man, I think these women
to be my sisters,
            Geneviève Bergeron
            Hélène Colgan
            Natalie Croteau
            Barbara Daigneault
            Anne-Marie Edward
            Maud Haviernick
            Barbara Marie Kleuznick
            Maryse Leclair
            Maryse Leganière
            Anne-Marie Lemay
            Sonia Pelletier
            Michèle Richard
            Annie St-Arneault
            Annette Turcotte

PSALMS

BY THE BIRD-BATH

...because you are lukewarm, neither
hot nor cold, I am about to spit you
out of my mouth.   Revelation 3:16

This hush is of snowflakes
trying to make up their minds—
hang in there together quilting
white on white or disperse liquidly?
        Sister squirrel flounces up
to the counter of my bird-bath
where bartender January
hesitates between ice and water

All this havering climatology
all this middle-of-the-roading
along the rim of winter
induces qualms in me about my text
which pronounces lukewarm dangerous:
am I collecting like sour saliva
in the mouth of God to be spat out?
        for my barometer
generally reads *via media*, the odd
typhoon only serving to define my zone
as temperate, some might say tepid
        and a lot of folk
in Dante who didn't have the chutzpah
to sin as if they meant it seem familiar

Seductive with risk, hotrod zealots
and apostles of cool zoom by me
driving under the influence, as I try
to steer down the edge of middle
with some passion

Heck, I barely have
breath enough to sound the toot of ordinary

Nevertheless I and you too
sister squirrel are probably OK
for now
            between us we can
plead not guilty of lukewarm:
            your heart beats hot
with various diurnal thrills
of staying alive and I am cold
inside my suit of skin

God will not spit us out today

THE CATCH
Luke 5

It wasn't as if we didn't know about those types.
We'd had itinerant preachers before,
all kinds, all with the gift of gab:
professional cultists, front men
for Galilean separatists, miracle men
blarneying the hair off warts
or laying the fear of God on boils,
then voices down at end of day
to catch a bowl of fish and lentils.

Then this one came. Andrew swore right off
that he must be Messiah. Oho! in your dreams!
we had messiah alarms regular as herring runs.
But he was different. That authority.
I'd never let a stranger use my boat before,
I owned the damn thing but I felt as if...
as if the Owner had arrived. And that catch—
as if every last fish in the sea was struggling
to pop its eyes and flap its tail for him.
"OK preacher", I'd said, humouring him,
"we'll let the nets down if you say so."

That was the last time, let me tell you,
I ever thought he needed humouring.
No bait but his word and in no time at all
both boats swamping with his weight of fishlore.
Pungent with slime and slithering in his catch
I quavered like a sprat before the Pike of Pikes
(it wasn't so much the fear of being eaten
as feeling so junior)—his laughter reeled us in:
"Don't be scared", he said, "come,
come with me, let's fish for souls".

166

He had me landed then, although
I didn't always understand, especially
when he let those bigwigs get their hooks in him.
They skinned him, strung him in the sun to dry
while we sank back into the swim
of old times, anonymous in Galilee again—
or tried to, but he was much too good a fisher:
having gutted death for breakfast
he'd risen early and was present, emerging
solid from the mist of our despair.

He let me easy off my hook: three gentle pulls,
once for each time I'd tried, that dreadful cockcrow,
to cough him from my gullet. Since then his catch
has grown and praises him on many shores.
I understand more, now. Those loaves, those fishes,
how he shares himself. How he casts
with heaven's own skill and patience on the waters
of God's world. Now in this Roman prison
I remember, suddenly, those teeming, swamping boats,
me half drowned in a thrash of scales
but rising to the lure of his word:
"Don't be scared", he said, "come,
come with me, let's fish for souls".

DO NOT WAIT
Matthew 25:31-46

Do not wait for the Last Judgement.
It takes place every day.
                    Albert Camus

The Rapture remains, friends,
in its postponement mode
Do not wait, burn those calories
of anticipation in studying
to pass charity's unscheduled exams,
her snap quizzes
                    Rapturizing
is beside the point—that point
of seraph-charged mundanity
which serves, any moment, peremptory
summons to its everyday assizes:
next session of this here,
                        this right now
judgement unplanned, irreversible

Leave those storied sheep and goats,
ambered in their parable, to heaven.
Leave out-of-this-world punishments,
leave ecstasies of the end rumbling and
flickering below apocalyptic horizons.
Attend to the middle of our narrative:
        A cup of water given irrigates
whole acres of the scalding sands of hell
        A right-hand slice of pizza not knowing
what its left-hand cup of coffee's up to
will sing among Christ's loaves and fishes
        Give a coat and sweater, hear
Satan's molars break for gnashing

Charity—we are talking love-in-action—
can be calculated, customary
but in good faith,
                    can be as regular
as seasons but true
                    can be impulsive—
even to stepping on some toes
of self-esteem—but genuine
                    Spare some compassion
but no sympathy or credence
for that cheap exsanguinated sneer
        bleeding heart
        just a bleeding heart
because
a heart that remembers how to bleed
is a heart still living, beating
apocalypse is now, yes now, yes now

DRIVEN FAR INTO THE DESERT
Psalm for Lent

Driven far into the desert,
burning, day is burning there
wilderness of ridge and gully
freezing, night is freezing there
       Careful, Jesus, please take care
       thirst and hunger are both near
Satan basking like a scorpion
tempting, he is tempting there:
Yes, you'll get to choose who's evil
crush them, yes, and crush them there
       Careful, Jesus, please take care
       hate is lurking somewhere near
Good's a power to be asserted
righteous, you'll be righteous there
yes and all the world will follow
love you, yes, and love you there
       Careful, Jesus, please take care
       pride is out and hunting near
Set the face to city southward
wonders, signs and wonders there
O Jerusalem! how often
prophets preaching, preaching there
       Careful, Jesus, please take care
       Law and Order know you're near
Will a donkey do for triumph?
Shouting, happy shouting there
but for disappointed zealots
anger, mortal anger there
       Careful, Jesus, please take care
       troops approaching, they are here

DRY BONE VALLEY
Ezekiel 37:1-14

It's like trying to stay upright,
scorched and breathless in the blast
of some coughing rot-toothed dragon.

Yahweh, this guided tour is tough going.
As vistas go, it's in questionable taste—hills
bare ribbed and drought-dried to the bone;

Satan plays Lego with Rwandan skeletons,
chews over the remains of hope in Darfur
and a thousand other slums:

such pornography of desolation—
Yahweh, can these bones live?
how have we been brought to this?

We wait on you. Do not press *rewind*,
returning things only to the way they were.
Do something, plant something new in us,

reassemble the strewn backbones
of our resolve, breathe prophecy into us
so that blade by blade, tuft by tuft

we may animate these lenten slopes
with living green of easter hopes.

DUE TIME
Matthew 19:16-22

Some dream of milking
the Roman occupation
for a fortune
                    others of kicking
imperial ass and/or reciting
all five books of Psalms by heart
                    I dream—
perhaps no more modestly—of
living without contradictions, of not
making a special case of myself
                    Not for me
exemption-riddled Torah—just a few
emergency loopholes, time-honoured,
and maybe the odd tooth mark of practice
on the unscrolling theory of my life:
                    I keep the Law

That wandering rabbi attracted me.
For people like him compromise is
a euphemism for contradiction.
                    Price for admission
to his vocation was prohibitively simple:
"liquidate your assets, distribute all
proceeds among the poor, follow me."
Now *there's* radical surgery enough
for every compromise
                    I hesitated,
I understood of course that travelling
without contradictions means travelling light,
but the best of my baggage was people—
human treasure, dependent, non-convertible
to alms for beggars

He turned to his
disciples, went his way, not one to wait
(not then, anyway, not there) while I stood
trying to reckon up moral accounts

Till recently I've lived a compromise,
contradiction—whatever—doing well
in my affairs the better to help poor
people help themselves the better

He is long gone, but now
a certain time seems to have come due
and I am free to pay my full admission

to his persisting vocation
                    I feel
neither blamed nor justified, just
curious still:
                    What time was due
back then at that place, that moment
when he liked me but left me
with all these years of wondering?

HERE IN THIS GARDEN
Mark 14:32-50

Here in this garden called Gethsemane
with moonlight silvering old olive trees
hope wavers, struggling to discern the way:
await events? or best to slip away?
Things once seemed clear so why this fierce unease
with friends perplexed, an anxious company?

Although this garden called Gethsemane
stirs cooling in a drowsy midnight breeze,
the anguished sweat of choosing tastes like blood;
hope gasps and flails in a despairing flood
how can I *know* God's will with mine agrees?
No help from friends—a sleepy company

The lower groves of dear Gethsemane
are flickering now but not with fireflies
Sleep while you can, friends, but they're almost here
A kiss, a scuffle, shouts, a bloody ear,
hope gutters under mercenary eyes
and night engulfs a scattered company

HIP HIP HOSANNA!
Mark 11

Hip Hip Hosanna!
Chip off David's block!
if you ever need an agent
       let me know
just call on me, because
you're bound to need
good press and image management

Hip Hip Hosanna!
Greetings, Jesus down from north,
if you ever need a reference
       let me know
just call on me, because
they're bound to ask
all about your moral fitness

Hip Hip Hosanna!
Well, god-struck Galilean,
if you ever need a funeral
       let me know
just call on me, because
we're bound to give
even far outs decent burial

I GAZE OUT
Matthew 7

I gaze out through my splintered eye
blinking my silly raft of planks along
and hardly see for looking
at specks in other people's eyes

we bump: more slivers in each other's eye
I splutter righteous looks about—
how blind people are! steering
their damn rafts into the way I see things

O Christ! tip over the whole daft contraption
of my wooden gaze, roll me under,
press me down in your good measure full
and running over, dunk me in your point of view

so when I surface I can clearly see
how you eased my eye of two big planks
hoisted them, crosswise, on your shoulder
stumbled them up some provincial hill of bones
and mounted them: a speck on two terrific sticks
hanging in the shocked sun's eye

so when—O Christ be merciful—
I dare to lift my gaze again
I can watch your awful splinter
so root, so flower in love's passion
so grow into the apple of God's eye
that I can share unlumbered looks
with all these friends, feast easy
with them and you, here, together,
in its compassionate shade

I'M PRAYING IN JOPPA
Acts 11

I'm praying in Joppa when I have this dream
a sheet full of creatures who aren't what they seem
each is unique, not a one of them unclean
they are all God's creatures let down from heaven
> *this is where my learning begins*
> *let that sheet stretch over my sins*

I say: God, look what you've let down in your sheet
welfare mums, delinquents, and many a deadbeat—
God says: Listen up runt, that's no way to greet
any of my creatures let down from heaven
> *this is where my hearing begins*
> *let that sheet stretch over my sins*

I say: But this lot you've let down in your sheet
they're foreign and shifty, they sponge, lie and cheat
God says: *Your* little secrets don't smell too sweet
so lay off my children let down from heaven
> *this is where my seeing begins*
> *let that sheet stretch over my sins*

I say: Check out that crowd let down in your sheet
dealers, freaked out sickos, queers I'd hate to meet—
God says: You need help and though hardly a treat
you're one of my creatures let down from heaven
> *this is where my healing begins*
> *let that sheet stretch over my sins*

JOURNEYING
Acts 9:1-19

There rides angry Saul on his high horse
        Oh yes, how the miles trot by
shouts threats and direments until he's hoarse
        Oh yes, how miles trot trot by

Flare of a vision blindingly bright
        Oh yes, how time slows right down
now his soul sees but his eyes lose sight
        Oh yes, how his time slows down

Voice in the light, *Stop! you're hurting me*
        Oh yes, how that Word can sting
Paul's your name now, go preach about me
        Oh yes, how that Word does ring

Trust me, your eyes will be undazzled
        Oh yes, how time moves again
Make friends with those you got so frazzled
        Oh yes, how things flow again

Braving gentile seas goes sailor Paul
        Oh yes, how the waves roll high
weather-beaten apostle to all
        Oh yes, how the waves rock by

LAZARUS
John 11

I have never felt so queer
out of breath, friends, out of breath
such an ill man you have here
sick to death Oh sick to death

pray for Jesus to appear
will he come Oh will he come?
too late, too late now, I fear
gone all numb, friends, gone all numb

doctor turns to pack his gear
hope is passed Oh hope is passed
how you weep but I can't hear
ebbing fast, friends, ebbing fast

gates of life close firm and sheer
as I leave, friends, as I leave
brother Jesus drops a tear
Martha weep, O Mary grieve

tone familiar, sound so clear
such a voice Oh such a voice
Jesus rousing my dead ear
brain turns on, friends, bones rejoice

stumbling out to face good cheer
all unwound Oh all unwound
propped between two sisters dear
lost and found, friends, lost and found

LENTEN PSALM

The winter of Toronto town is come
it settles in my very marrow

I shiver on Queen and Jarvis corner
I make my bed on warm air-vents

It is not easy to give thanks for charity
the bread of poverty is very bitter

An orchestra plays in the mall
but I am not allowed to loiter

O God, I ache in your chilly absence
please, please shine your countenance upon me

sound your horn of saving plenty in my ear
warm me with some hope so I can praise you

ORACLES
Numbers 22:7-35

Three times Balaam whacked me.
Three times, the old fart.
Me! faithful as sunrise for years.

So maybe I did turn off the road
(bolted into a field if truth be known)
but what would you do if you saw
an angel touch down in the middle of the road,
armed and dangerous?
                          Thwack
So maybe I did try to turn round
on that knee-knocking path (scraping B's foot
against the vineyard wall if truth be known)
but what would you do if you saw
an angel covering the path from zig to zag,
armed and dangerous?
                          Thwack
So on that final trickle of a one-way track
maybe I did do a despairing flop under Balaam
(jarring his coccyx if truth be known)
but what would you do if you saw
an angel spill acres of light over every inch of track,
armed and dangerous?
                          Thwack
But I had my day, hee-ohyes-haw.
        Just imagine—
angel with knuckles big as silver oranges,
my God-opened mouth speaks its own oracle,
Balaam sees the light at last, hears the angel
tell him I saved his life by bolting off that road.

If ever I could, I'd utter another oracle:
We folk lower down the food chain
often serve God better in our ways
than you do in yours, so take note
when we baulk: there might be an angel
standing in the middle of your road,
armed and dangerous

THE SAMARITAN CONNECTION

1. THE OTHER SIDE
Luke 10:25-37

He loads his donkey with his plans
and sets out on his laden day

Some are born neighbourly, some
have neighbourliness thrust upon them
like now, on this bend in the road
from Jerusalem to Jericho,
where excuses multiply like flies
feeding on his schedule of commitments,
zooming around his tight timetable—
　　　　pass by, they buzz,
　　　　pass by on the other side

Much later, before the Bar, glum
on Judgement Day he listens
to the Accuser's impressive recitation
of his sins and failures, then
hears the Judge pronounce:

In heaving
that half-dead man up onto his donkey
the defendant heaved up me.
Just as that soothing oil and cleansing wine
blest the traveller's beat-up flesh,
so were they balm to mine.
Also,
the innkeeper's evidence is reliable and clear

There is no case to answer.
Welcome to the neighbourhood, Samaritan.
Mr Prosecutor, you may stand down
and pass by on the other side.

2. WOMAN AT THE WELL
John 4:4-30; 39-42

I'm Peter. I remember you. You graduated
from your first body recently? *This morning*
I think. So I'll go with a 'Good Morning' then.
I was only pretending to look for your name
in this tome—something I sometimes do
just in case that's what newcomers expect.

Now then: Five husbands and a live-in boy-friend.
A bit short on family values? *Husbands! One just*
vanished. Two died young and poor. Two who often
slapped me around then threw me out. No claim
to any house or land, no sons for my old age.
Story of my life: no security, no family, no prospects.

Number six is…was toy-boy and parttime pimp.
I dropped him after I met a man who came across
like Messiah—say! weren't you one of the men
there that day? Such embarrassment! what shame!
you guys hardly knew where to look: a Samaritan—
a woman yet! Yes, astonishment and scant respect—

not the first or last time I floundered clueless
in his wake. *I followed along after that Yeshua*
but things fell apart, right from the moment when
those villagers, my gallant neighbours, became
even more holier-than-thou once they'd seen and
heard him for themselves. Talk about disrespect.

I've often thought about him and his 'living water'.
He's somewhere around. *What! he made it here?*
Yes, a…glorified version—anyway, a leading citizen.
You can drink your fill together, and don't blame
those village folk too much. No matter what,
you evangelized the lot of them as I recollect.

SEVENTY TIMES SEVEN
Matthew 18:21-22

I try not to sweat the heavy stuff
that some spend their lives refusing
to forgive
        That sound of the universe
unfolding as it should includes
the note of not owing me a thing
        I've learned to read
and the fine print on my birthright
says not a word about free passes
or unlimited entitlement
        Though it smells good
I resist sniffing the dizzy glue
of injured merit
        For the rest, seventy
times seven sounds like a lot
of forgiving.
        Seasoned expert in the need
to be forgiven, I am mere amateur
in forgiving, there being so little
to forgive—bad mouthed here and there,
overcharged once or twice, occasionally
short-changed as to apologies and/or
obligations due
                But even if I were done
some wrong monstrous as Beelzebub
and had to empty the whole 70 x 7 account
just to approach forgiving, both Peter's question
and Jesus' answer seem a bit easy, a shade pat
        for when I alone am wronged I,
with my full belly and so far unplundered pension
get to regulate my own micro-economy
of to forgive or not

But what if
my wronged population of one
is multiplied to the second…third…
fifth power?
        Who forgives
on behalf of all demeaned Ontarians
those savage Tory antics at Queen's Park?
        Who forgives the murders of
King, Ghandi, Romero, Allende,
in their names?

        Leaving the bad guys to heaven
doesn't cut it, so will any laureates
in juridical theology and/or macro-
economics of forgiveness in the house
please step up?

Retribution is fitted for judge's robes;
punishment holds the eye-for-eye brief
in opinion's court;
        Law&Order bustles in
to plead conundrums: How to calculate
remission, restitution, restoration
in the plural without rigging
or ignoring justice? without leading her
by the nose tenderly as asses are?

Fine tuning Truth Commissions
is unearthly difficult, but
in pandemics of massacre, hallowed
vengeance, homeric corruption
and dynastic grudges there is hope
for both the doers and the done to
only in the unfamiliar pangs of truth-
telling mercies freely exchanged—

mercies *now*, not
in some all-purpose afterlife,
for God's unplumbed compassion
wells up most healing in the mercy
we allow each other here, when
forgiveness is not code for doing nothing
　　　　and it becomes thinkable
for hands rinsed in mercy to write
forgiveness as a paragraph of justice

Perhaps after all question and answer
were not too easy, not so pat:
　　　　it might be
that 70 x 7 is gospel code for
try to make a habit of difficult mercy

TERRORIST
Psalm 139:15-16

True, Dr Donne, I am a little world
made cunningly, routinely practicing
Nobel-class chemistries, filing
a trillion reality-bytes an hour
and twirling sub-atomic galaxies
without undue trepidations
for some time now
              And me too, Walt,
I contain multitudes I know,
but if Christ within is generalissimo
of all my genes, what I do not know,
what bothers me is where this zealot
comes from
              Elusive as truth, suddenly
he's there looking through my eyes

Is he neuron of my neurons? DNA
of my DNA? this fundamentalist,
this worst of terrorists, debauchee
of certainty?—versed in mayhem,
mostly biblical, he wields his patents
on what's what like laser guns
Who will deliver me from him?
O God, finish this psalm for me,
permit me to imagine you saying:
I, love who moves the sun
and other stars—not to mention
the zodiacs of your inner space—
made you, terrorist and all
              there is no
quackery for saving you from you
whom I will be reconfiguring one day

as next rhythm of your dance in me
my dance in you
                    meanwhile
love me with all five wits
and—you know the moves—
your neighbour as yourself
                    which
should fetch your terrorist you
by his shadowy scruff of neck
and fade him into some daylight
of uncertainties negotiated calmly
among deeds of charity

THOMAS
John 20

I shall be set down, no doubt, as doubting Thomas;
       the hat fits well enough and I will wear it.
Sometimes in these Keralan dawns I recall
       how hard assurance was to come by

For a terrible few days I thought that Jesus
       was one more would-be messianic has-been,
some charismatic moth cynically squashed
       between religious and colonial politicians

Assurance remains an erratic weekend guest
       so "doubting Thomas" let it stay,
even though I am the farthest sent evangel
       and our Indian Jesus-movement thrives

The faith I find myself sustained in
       has little to do with certainty,
much less with signing covenants, observance
       of law's letter, zealous formulas

It is a gift and blest indeed are they
       who, without seeing, go on trusting;
they sip hope's cup of nourishment,
       graced beyond all seeing is believing

But I, Thomas Didymus, apostle,
       shall remain a willing sign of doubt
because that sign marks what faith I do have
       as generous, open-handed act of grace

TWO TAKES ON RAPHAEL/AZARIA'S ADVICE
A king's secrets ought to be kept, but the works
of God should be acknowledged publicly.
The Book of Tobit 12:7

A shortage of kings does not mean
there are no secrets to be kept;
besides, we have a queen who must have
a secret or two left in spite of the media's
bottomless hypocrisies about we-the-public's
right to know and their cynical massacre
of royal privacies.
Statecraft,
our text purports, is owed certain silences,
some prudent discretions that go with
the management of human affairs.
There are of course
secrets that are deadly or go gangrenous
in the keeping. And of course there are
legislative assemblies that know rather less
than a troop of baboons about prudent
discretions or the rhetorics of silence.
But there is
no call to afford the godhead courtesies
of decorous silence, no need to be
discreet about the works of God,
whose Alpha-Omega privacy is inviolable,
who is immune to identity-theft though
assorted sects keep trying.

Hence let us praise the set of sun
on Lawrence Avenue West,
let us bless the rise of moon
over Lawrence Avenue East.

191

Let us give thanks for old stands
of red pine, for the muskeg and
outrider larches escorting the Abitibi,
Mattagami, Albany, and Attawapiskat
on their run towards James Bay;
                    for caribou
lumbering unannounced across
Highway 480 in Newfoundland,
                    for icebergs
anchored off Chance Islands and
the perfect keyhole harbour of St John's;
                    for Fundy tides,
for Breton Narrows, Grand and Little.

Let us bless the fructuous embrace
of Saskatchewan river's arms, North
and South, beneath the uncluttered
skylight of Canada's vast house.

Let us praise L'Isle-aux-Coudres,
tidal flats of Kamouraska, not forgetting
Rivière du Saint-Maurice or Gaspésie.

Let us give thanks for Cypress Hills,
for Fraser Canyon, Lake Celestine,
Clayquot, the elevation of Mount Logan.

With trepidations and attested caveats
let us even bless ourselves, work of God's sixth day.

*

The mandate of Mr Justice Gomery
is no doubt called for, but it also whets
our appetite for ghoulish revelation,

192

hence a gust of prophesying shakes me,
an urge insists: Royal or not, some secrets
should be kept. So I will take up station

in Dundas Square and fall to prophecy
with just my sign, MUM'S THE WORD—no leaflets,
no devices of amplification;

my secrets are safe despite contumely,
I'm proof against all hostile epithets—
no prophet's honoured in his own nation.

Now God, stand up for fellows such as I,
being discreet's in very short supply.

NOTES

NOTES

(p. 1-2) *Addendum to* **A Primer…:** Quotations are from *Timon of Athens,* Act I, scenes iii and iv; *Dombey and Son*, conclusions to chapters 41 and 8; W.B.Yeats' poem *Byzantium*.

(p.8-9) *Christmas Tidings*: **Elizabeth Schüssler Fiorenza** (b.1938), a feminist theologian, biblical scholar, author of such works as *Bread Not Stone* (1984) and *Discipleship of Equals* (1998).

(p.17-8) *In-House Glosa*: **"In-House"** because the initial four lines of a proper glosa are from the work of an author other than the one who writes the following ten-line stanzas. See P.K.Page, *Hologram: a book of glosas*, (Brick Books, 1994) for fine examples of the genre. *Hologram* was reprinted in Volume 2 of P.K.Page's *The Hidden Room: Collected Poems* (The Porcupine's Quill, 1997).

(p.29) *Spring*: **"…makes a pulpit..",** refers to the equestrian statue of Edward VII in Queen's Park, Toronto.

(p.30-1) *Summer*: **"Et in Arcadia ego"** (31). Arcadia: an actual district in Greece but ever since the 2nd century BCE it has been appropriated by literature and the visual arts and developed as a highly idealized place where shepherds, or sometimes fisher folk lead simple pastoral lives in rustic, usually idyllic surroundings. But it has never been all innocent fun and games in Arcadia. From its beginnings as a subject of the arts there have been, as with Eden, intimations of suffering and mortality in Arcadia. The Latin phrase permits various nuances of meaning but is usually rendered as "I am present even in Arcadia"—with the human condition of mortality, or death itself, as the implied speaker.

(p.41-2) *Stanley Spencer's* **"John Donne…":** This

was Spencer's (d.1959) first publicly exhibited painting (1912) when he was nineteen. At the time his reading included the sermons of John Donne (1571?-1631) and to some extent Spencer's painting is in conversation with a sermon (ca.1623) that speaks of "going to heaven by heaven", which Spencer took to mean travelling to heaven alongside heaven. "He had this idea", his brother Gilbert reported, that heaven was right alongside: when "...walking along the road he turned his head and looked into Heaven, in this case part of Widbrook Common." The epigraph of this poem is from another Donne sermon (1625/26) that Spencer could just as well have been at the time. So the rhetorical situation here is that the speaker in the poem is in three way engagement—with Spencer's painting and two fragments from Donne's sermons.
Widbrook Common (41) is near Cookham, a village in Berkshire, England where Spencer was born and lived a good part of his life. **Cardinal Bellarmine** (1562-1621): a leading Jesuit of the Counter-Reformation. Early in his career Donne was for a time what we might call a research assistant for the Anglican Bishop of London who was embroiled in religious polemics with, among others, Cardinal Bellarmine. **Rosemary Radford Ruether** (42) noted feminist theologian whose books include *Sexism and God-Talk* and *New Heaven/New Earth*.
"..[P]reaching from a cloud though in none": Izaak Walton's *Life of Dr John Donne* (1640) is very much of a 'saint's life' but is nevertheless full of good things, such as this striking image of Donne preaching.

(**p.50**) *The Stink of Experience*: **Castiglione** (1478-1529) Italian writer, courtier, and diplomat whose very popular *Book of the Courtier* (1528) develops nonchalance and the art of appearing effortlessly artless as essential, natural seeming attributes of the good courtier.

(**p.51-2**) *Il faut imaginer Sisyphe heureux*: Because he

persisted in flouting their authority the gods of ancient Greek myth condemned Sisyphus to forever push a heavy stone up a hill, only to have it forever rolling right back down. **Danaë** (51), also from Greek myth, was seduced by Zeus who, for that particular conquest, took the form of a shower of gold. **Albert Camus** (1913-60), a French intellectual: novelist, playwright, and essayist. His famous essay *The Myth of Sisyphus* is a quintessentially existentialist piece. (See also the epigraph of poem on p.168.)

(**p.68-9**) *Among Bruckner Fans*: Anton **Bruckner** Austrian composer (1824-1896). **Lent police,** special constables hired to enforce city regulations against buying, selling, and eating meat during Lent. A **standing tuck** (69) is a rapier standing upright on its point; see Shakespeare's *Henry IV*, Part One, Act II where the grossly fat Falstaff uses this image of extreme skinniness as the climax of his slanging match with Prince Hal. Denise **Levertov** (1923-97), a major American poet whose body of work included a number of haikus, or haiku-esque pieces like this tiny perfect insight into the character and works of Bruckner.

(**p.72**) *Nocturne: Shandong Camelot*: "…**open man- slaughter and bold bawdrie**", was Roger Ascham's considered opinion of a selection of Arthurian legends as rendered by Thomas Malory (d.1471). Ascham (1515-68), a good example of 16th century Christian humanism in England, was for a while private tutor to Elizabeth I.

(**p.75**) *Nile Rhythms*: In his *Vocation of the Poet* the great poet Rainer Maria Rilke (1875-1926) recalls a sight on the Nile during a visit to Egypt: a boat is moving to the strokes of a large group of rowers; up front, facing them, a drummer beats out the pace; in front of him, right up on the prow and facing *forward*, a singer sings future-ward, towards the boat's destination.

(**p.84-91**) *Mercy Jones Suite*: In the second verse
(89) of part [5] Mercy recalls the closing words of Act
IV, scene i of Shakespeare's *King Henry V*; in the third
verse she recalls, but puts her own spin on, William
Wordsworth's finely contemptuous phrase in his "Pre-
face to the Second Edition of *Lyrical Ballads*" (1800).

(**p.94-7**) *Glimpses*: This gist of this curse, "**I tell you,
churlish Turks**..." (96) is borrowed from *Hamlet,* Act
V, scene 2.

(**p.101-4**) *Roving Reporter*: **PNAC** (102) Project for
a New American Century, a virulent imperialist strain of
the doctrine of Manifest Destiny; **CSIS** i.e. Canadian
Security Intelligence Service.

(**p.116-19**) *Ornithology 101*: **Parliament of Fowls**
(117) is the title of a poem in the love-vision genre by
Geoffrey Chaucer (c.1343-1400); in the 'vision' section
of the poem the characters are birds.

(**p.155-6**) *That Thin Man*: Eli Mandel made use of
the phrase "**silent speaking words**" (156) which
comes from Tennyson's *In Memoriam* XCV and no
doubt derives ultimately from Psalm 19:3-4.

(**p.185-7**) *Seventy Times Seven*: "...**leading her ten-
derly by the nose as asses are**" (186) echoes Iago's
words just before the conclusion of *Othello*, Act I.

(**p.188**) *Terrorist*: One of Donne's penitential sonnets
[5] opens with "**I am a little world made cunningly..**";
"**..love that moves the sun and other stars...**" comes
from Book III, Canto 33 of *Paradiso*, the conclusion of
of Dante's *Commedia*, or *Divine Comedy.*

(**p.191-3**) *Two Takes on Raphael/Azaria's Advice:*
Early in 2004 **Mr Justice Gomery** (192) was appointed
to preside over a Commission of Inquiry into the alleged
fiscal mismanagement and improper use of funds by mem-
bers of the federal Liberal Party establishment in Quebec.